Free Speech on Campus

Free Speech on Campus

Sigal R. Ben-Porath

PENN

UNIVERSITY OF PENNSYLVANIA PRESS

PHILADELPHIA

Publication of this volume was aided by funds donated in honor of Martin Meyerson, University president (1970–81) and chairman of the Press's board of trustees (1984–97).

Published by
University of Pennsylvania Press
Philadelphia, Pennsylvania 19104-4112
www.upenn.edu/pennpress

Printed in the United States of America

A Cataloging-in-Publication record is available from the Library of Congress

Cover design by John Hubbard

ISBN 978-0-8122-5007-7 hardcover
ISBN 978-0-8122-9492-7 ebook

Contents

Preface

My phone buzzed just as I finished cooking dinner. The voice on the other end of the line told me that I had to return to work right away. I am not a first responder; I am a professor of education and philosophy. Yet in the midst of the crisis of the moment, I was urgently needed on campus.

A group of students had staged a sit-in at the University of Pennsylvania's administration building, demanding changes to the school's investment portfolio to bring it into better alignment with their ideology. "The building closes at 6:00 p.m.," my staff liaison told me, "but the students are planning to stay overnight."

Minutes later, in my work clothes once again, I was on my way back to campus. It was the end of my second year as the chair of the university's Committee on Open Expression. I could nearly recite from memory the guidelines intended to protect free speech on Penn's campus. Developed in the late 1960s after a spate of student protests, the guidelines were designed to make sure that views are not suppressed based on their content and that during demonstrations the campus can continue to function as an environment in which all have the opportunity to learn, teach, and conduct research (or simply go about their daily business without severe disruption). The students planning to continue their protest overnight were in violation of the requirement that demonstrations be conducted in a way that does not disrupt university operations or put their own safety at risk.

The next two days were a blur of negotiations and delivered pizzas and working with administrators and security to make sure that the students who stayed overnight would be safe and that offices would be secure; that the free speech of the students would be protected while the university operated as smoothly as possible; and that student leaders understood that, as long as they were in violation of university policies, it was unlikely that their demands would be seriously considered, especially when meeting those demands would require long-term policy changes. At the end of two days, the students left without incident and with assurances that the debate with university officials about their group's goals would continue, as it does with all student groups.

Far from being a particularly exciting or noteworthy incident, this sit-in was commonplace—and far more representative of free speech tensions on college campuses than most of the more widely publicized events discussed in this book. Yes, a handful of high-profile cases have culminated in disinvitations, violent clashes, and ousted speakers. But more often, controversies surrounding free speech on campus involve negotiation and debate among multiple parties that generally seek the same goal: allowing or encouraging speech on matters of political and

2

civic importance while maintaining a constructive atmosphere for learning and research. That's primarily how I frame discussion of these issues in this book—as matters of inclusion and freedom.

In the pages that follow, I examine the current state of the arguments about free speech on campus, using real-world examples to explore the contexts in which conflicts erupt, as well as to assess the place of identity politics and concerns with safety and dignity within them. I offer a framework for thinking about free speech controversies both inside and outside the classroom, shifting the focus away from disputes about legality and harm and toward practical considerations linked to education and inclusion. I attempt to provide readers with strategies to de-escalate tensions and negotiate highly charged debates surrounding trigger warnings, safe spaces, and speech that verges on hate. My hope is that everyone with a stake in campus controversies—professors, students, administrators, and informed members of the wider public—will find value in my analysis of these vitally important issues.

In the first chapter, I survey the landscape of free speech on American campuses today by way of several illustrative examples. I outline some of the current tools used by colleges to protect free speech and to respond to challenges and tensions in this domain, and I begin to dispel some common myths about free speech on campus.

The second chapter develops a framework for inclusive freedom in response to the changing mission of higher education institutions in the United States. I show how speech practices and protections can be tailored to respond to this changing mission and to diversifying student and faculty bodies on campus without detracting from democratic commitments. The protection of free speech in an educational institution can and should be treated as an imperative, yet it also needs to be expressed in flexible ways that can respond to new and evolving challenges related to speech. Here I discuss arguments about limiting speech to prevent hurtful statements from harming vulnerable students and argue that the suppression of speech is not a productive or democratic response to the risk of harm. I also suggest responses to concerns about harm that stop short of censorship and silencing.

Chapter 2 also clarifies why I reject the tension commonly emphasized in the free speech debate between inclusion and freedom. The diversity of the student body, as well as diversity within the campus community as a whole, is an opportunity for individuals to learn and for the university to expand its mission, which involves an inclusive, open-minded, and broad search for truth. This mission has a civic dimension, one that prepares students to participate in democratic politics beyond the bounds of the university as conscious and committed members of their local communities and the wider world. Protecting students' well-being within and beyond the classroom is only the first necessary step toward achieving this goal. As long as students' sense of belonging and safety is ensured, the campus should consciously support their efforts to voice their views and form alliances and connections beyond their immediate affinity and identity groups. As they grow to participate in the broader public sphere that the campus represents, students learn valuable lessons about how to act as responsible democratic citizens after they graduate.

Contents

In the third chapter, I consider the place of identity politics in the debate about free speech on campus, especially in the context of the activities of student groups. I consider intellectual and dignitary harms and how the campus can prevent or respond to them without suppressing speech while providing access for all members to the activities and learning that take place on the quad and around campus. I argue that the demand for civility is not a useful way to frame the interactions of students on campus and instead suggest ways in which the concept of inclusive freedom can be applied to the teeming activity that takes place every day in and around the college quad.

Chapter 4 moves from the quad to the classroom. I offer ways to protect the speech and access of all students in class, once again by rejecting the norm of civility as the sole framework for organizing classroom interactions. Instead, I suggest norms of expression that can be used by instructors and students alike, along with ways these norms might best be organized and protected—while also keeping in mind that learning, and therefore intellectual candor and a commitment to truth, is the primary aim of classroom speech.

In the conclusion, I suggest ways in which some of the cases discussed throughout the book could have been resolved if addressed using the concept and norm of inclusive freedom. I close with practical suggestions for students and student groups, instructors, and campus leaders who wish to preserve inclusive freedom on college campuses today.

The State of the Debate

The liberal commitment to an open-minded atmosphere on campus has been largely embraced by students and faculty for generations, yet groups with a variety of ideological leanings are threatening this commitment and atmosphere today. Some groups seek to limit debates on subjects such as race, sexuality, war, and international politics so as to prevent the expression of views they believe to lie beyond the bounds of reasonable discussion; other groups seek to instigate fights over the limits of free speech by inviting speakers who push these boundaries. Media scrutiny invites outsiders, especially right-wing politicians, to treat these tensions as evidence that colleges are indoctrinating rather than educating American youth, which then becomes an occasion to threaten public colleges and universities with funding cuts.

This chapter presents the current public and scholarly debates surrounding free speech on campus. The debate is marked by student bodies divided by their views toward speech protections, with some students demanding that administrators curtail free speech to protect vulnerable groups from harm, while others demand the liberty to hear and express unpopular opinions. At times, tensions flare beyond peaceful protests and circulated petitions, with speakers alleged to be harmful shouted down or even attacked.

This chapter lays out the contours of the current debate by way of an examination of some cases that touch on safe spaces, racial tensions, trigger warnings, and controversial speakers. I consider common views about what should drive and limit speech on campus, including a commitment to the First Amendment that overrides any need for unique considerations related to colleges and universities, contrasted with a commitment to diversity and inclusion (sometimes derided as a politically correct, or PC, vision) that is based on protecting all students from harm and hurt.

Free Speech Blues

Early in 2017, it seemed that civil discourse lost its footing and that free speech itself was rapidly becoming a matter of partisan politics in the United States. The Democratic insistence that "when they go low, we go high"[1] during the presidential campaign was quickly replaced by wide support for the punching of a white supremacist during a live television interview.[2] American campuses were not spared from these shifts. Colleges and universities hold a unique place in the conversation about speech, where they are seen as both the mirror of American democracy and the window into its future.

This is not the first era in American history when free speech was high on students' minds and spilling over to the public debate. Students were protesting the Vietnam War and the administration's policies in rowdy, sometimes violent marches nearly fifty years ago. At that time, civil rights struggles had a significant presence and impact on college campuses, and free speech—especially the students' right to object to the war or otherwise express unpopular views—was at the heart of the campus struggles. However, in the past few years, students are no longer as committed to free speech as they once were.

According to a recent survey, most American undergraduates believe First Amendment rights are secure.[3] At the same time, nearly half think some restrictions on free speech are justified. As the report accompanying the survey indicates, "Students do appear to distinguish controversial views from what they see as hate. They believe colleges should be allowed to establish policies restricting language and behavior that are intentionally offensive to certain groups, but not the expression of political views that may upset or offend members of certain groups."[4] These sentiments are echoed and the support for them is even stronger in the findings of an annual survey from UCLA.[5] Roughly 71 percent of this national sample of students agreed that schools should be allowed to place restrictions on offensive costumes and on racist or sexist speech on campus, up from 60 percent in the early 1990s.

For some commentators, especially on the right, this is a mark of political correctness, "snowflake" vulnerability, and an abdication of all that is right and good about American democracy.[6] Many on both the right and the left worry that the diminished value students attach to the protection of free speech indicates a dangerous slide toward authoritarian control of opinions or a retreat to comfort that relies on rejecting any view that might disrupt the orthodoxy of the day.[7]

These concerns, for the most part, are unwarranted. Clearly many students are young and have more to learn about the central importance of speech protection to the stability of a tolerant and open democracy and to the protection of minority views and groups. But generally the change of focus that they, as a generation, introduce into the debate is not one that should be of concern to the self-appointed guardians of democracy. Universities and colleges are institutions with aims that go well beyond the general goals of a democratic republic, and it makes sense for them to be organized and managed based on additional principles. Moreover, because they provide diverse educational contexts, colleges indeed should be concerned about inclusion and about actively creating a sense of connection and belonging. All this does not mean that free speech is unimportant for the research, learning, and civic missions of the university. It means, rather, that the implementation of free speech principles might reasonably look different on a college campus than it does in the town's square (whether real or virtual). Moreover, the fact that the main parties to the debate are young adults means that intense media scrutiny of their views and actions does little to support their process of developing and trying out ideas and views, including fringe ones, with the minimal consequence that an educational institution should be able to afford.

Still, some concern about these changes in students' positions seems warranted. While earlier generations saw free speech protections as necessary for allowing students to express their views, it is relatively common today for students to be open to some curtailment of speech for the purpose of protecting members of vulnerable groups who might be harmed by certain forms of expression. In this vein, a Middlebury student reflected after a free speech incident on her campus (discussed below), "For too long, a flawed notion of 'free speech' has allowed individuals in positions of power to spread racist pseudoscience in academic institutions, dehumanizing and subjugating people of color and gender minorities."[8] For students and others—mostly on the left—who espouse this view, "free speech" is another one of the master's tools, a lofty idea that helps people in power preserve their position while dismissing women as fitted mostly for domestic work, gay people as mentally ill, and racial minorities as intellectually inferior.

For free speech advocates, this argument is nothing but a politically correct effort to prevent anyone from voicing views that do not fall in line with a narrow "social justice" ideology. It is seen as a mark of weakness on the part of students who purportedly prefer support and protection over the intellectual courage that is required to explore new and different ideas. Or, as one conservative college professor proclaimed, "If we don't reverse this dangerous trend in our society there will soon be a majority of young people who will need to walk around in plastic bubble suits to protect them in the event that they come into contact with a dissenting viewpoint. That mentality is unworthy of an American."[9]

In between these two extreme positions, the one side calling to give up on free speech to protect vulnerable members and the other to protect free speech—and thus democracy—at all costs, a more nuanced debate has developed. Views from the scholarly debate are discussed in this book along with perspectives from different campuses, with the goal of developing a framework for inclusive freedom—an approach to free speech on campus that takes into account the necessity of protecting free speech in order to protect democracy and the pursuit of knowledge while recognizing the equal necessity of making sure that all are included in the ensuing conversation.

Why is free speech important at all for the work that colleges and universities are expected to do? Beyond its centrality to democracy, free speech allows institutions of higher education to fulfill their mission. It allows scholars and researchers to pursue and expand knowledge without fear, and it allows instructors to introduce new knowledge to younger generations to help them discover their own interests and develop their skills so that they can contribute to the same pursuits on campus or in various other jobs and positions. It enables students' civic organizations and other groups to express their views publicly and to exchange opinions with others. It also helps young people develop and try new ideas that can push democracy and society forward, even as they can be hard sometimes for adults (or fellow students) to accept.

Some of the most widely debated cases in the past few years generated two opposing possible responses—either you love free speech (and ridicule the vulnerable, whiny students who demand its curtailment) or you respect identity (and fume at First Amendment purists who, from their privileged ivory tower, refuse to recognize the power differences it creates). I begin by outlining some challenging recent cases, which show how the presumed opposition between protecting free speech and protecting vulnerable members of the community plays out on campuses today. The cases are outlined here, and some of them are discussed in more detail in the chapters that follow.

Halloween Costumes and Safe Spaces at Yale

Just before Halloween 2015, thirteen Yale administrators cosigned a letter that was sent out to the student body, suggesting that students should be cautious and sensitive about their choices for Halloween costumes and particularly advocating against costumes that could be seen as racist or expressing some inappropriate cultural appropriation. Erika Christakis, a lecturer, wrote a message in response, suggesting that colleges had gotten too cautious and that there should be room for students to make mistakes, to be obnoxious, and even to be a bit offensive. Some students were vehemently opposed to her position, which they saw as sanctioning racist expressions. After some testy public exchanges, an ongoing protest, and significant public attention, Erika Christakis resigned from Yale, and her husband, a professor and house dean, left his residential post. (I discuss this case in more detail in chapter 2.)

Struggling for Racial Equality in Missouri

In 2015, students at the University of Missouri established a group intent on exposing and bringing attention to discriminatory incidents on campus, especially those targeting African American students. They highlighted some troubling cases where slurs, swastikas, and verbal aggression were used against minority students and demanded a response from the administration. After they were rebuffed, the efforts escalated to include one student's hunger strike and—in a move that finally drew national attention and focused the administration's response—the university's mostly African American football team declared that it was going on strike. Ultimately, the university's president resigned, and some new initiatives were taken to try to remedy the issues raised by the students.[10] (I discuss this case in more detail in chapter 3.)

Rejecting Trigger Warnings in Chicago

In August 2016, before the start of the fall semester, University of Chicago's dean of students sent out a letter to all incoming students, stating that "Our commitment to academic freedom means that we do not support so-called 'trigger warnings,' we do not cancel invited speakers because their topics might prove controversial and we do not condone the creation of intellectual 'safe spaces' where individuals can retreat from ideas and perspectives at odds with their own."[11] A controversy ensued with both faculty and students raising concerns about the letter and the usual sides being taken by conservative and liberal commentators. (I return to this controversy at various points throughout the book.)

Chasing Away Controversial Speakers at Berkeley and Middlebury

The question of invited and disinvited speakers has become a focal point of the debate about free speech on campus as objections from student groups to the invitation of controversial speakers became more common and public starting in 2013–14. Robert B. Zoellick, the former president of the World Bank, withdrew as a commencement speaker at his alma mater, Swarthmore College, after students mounted a social media campaign calling him a "war criminal" because of his support of the 2003 war in Iraq. Students at Rutgers protested for similar reasons the invitation of Condoleezza Rice—hardly a controversial public figure—as commencement speaker, causing her to withdraw. Many other similar disagreements around speakers invited by colleges and by student groups continued to flare up in social and traditional media, with the usual laments voiced especially on the right about students' oversensitivity and close-mindedness. In 2017, the rising polarization around the country and on campuses nationwide drew intense media scrutiny to these events, which became part of the latest front in the culture wars. The UC-Berkeley student group Berkeley College Republicans invited Milo Yiannopoulos, the technology editor of the right-wing company Breitbart News, to give a speech on campus in February of 2017. Officials expressed their commitment to letting the event take place in the name of free speech, even as faculty members urged them to cancel the event. On the day of the event, student (and other) protestors took matters into their own hands, coordinating what turned out to be violent protests that included throwing smoke bombs, breaking windows, and starting fires. A few hours before the event started, it was canceled due to safety concerns, and the campus was placed on lockdown.[12] A university spokesman claimed that the violence that erupted was due to the actions of outsiders "implementing a very clear plan to engage in violence, disruption and property destruction."[13]

President Donald Trump weighed in on the events via Twitter, suggesting that if UC Berkeley didn't allow free speech, shown by canceling events such as this, they should no longer receive federal funds, to which a UC Regent, Gavin Newsom, replied, "As a UC Regent I'm appalled at your willingness to deprive over 38,000 students access to an education because of the actions of a few."[14] Berkeley's troubles did not end there, and the tensions around events, speakers, and protests continued to the chagrin of its administrators. "It feels like we've become the O.K. Corral for the Hatfield and McCoys of the right and left," said Dan Mogulof, the university's assistant vice chancellor for public affairs. "We're the venue for these showdowns taking place."[15]

Not long afterward, the Middlebury Enterprise Club invited Charles Murray for a presentation on his book *Coming Apart*. Known for his much-criticized 1994 book *The Bell Curve*, Murray's visit raised objections among students and faculty but was defended by the college administration as within the club's speech rights. The event was shut down by aggressive protesters. (I discuss these cases in more detail in chapter 3.)

The focus on cases that flame into public debate sometimes keeps other issues out of the conversation, and in this book I aim to bring them back in. In the Middlebury case, some protesters were physically violent—pushing, shoving, and even injuring the professor who hosted the event. This aspect of the case is not the main focus here because it is clearly a matter for police or criminal justice rather than for a principled discussion on free speech; the rest of this case—the invitation, the attempts to cancel the event, the protest, the administration's response—are all relevant and are further discussed below. The physical violence that erupted in Middlebury, the fires that were set on Berkeley's campus, death threats against African American students on Penn's campus—these are all indicative of rising tensions and polarization and, as such, are relevant to a discussion about speech on campus, but they mostly cannot be addressed by an appeal to norms and a reframing of the conversation (but rather by legal measures). Cases where property is defaced with swastikas or slurs and where hijabs are pulled off students' heads are heart-wrenching, but they are not the type of cases that can clarify how the conversation about speech needs to change.

In this book, I go beyond the focus on these widely discussed cases because they are limited in another way: they draw our attention away from the fact that most colleges, most of the time, resolve free speech issues through a fruitful, sometimes intense but still peaceful debate. The controversial speakers whose talks generated violent responses at Berkeley and Middlebury spoke at various other colleges in recent years with limited or no incidents.

On the same day that Murray spoke at Middlebury, Flemming Rose—the cartoonist whose depiction of the Prophet Muhammad resulted in riots—came to speak at Franklin and Marshall College (F&M). His talk drew strong emotions, a rally, and other forms of protest, but he spoke and engaged with the audience in a productive exchange. "There have been a number of social critics—in and outside of the academy—who have labeled an entire generation of students as illiberal crybullies," said Daniel R. Porterfield, president of F&M. "If you work at a college campus, you know that these sweeping denunciations are not accurate. Many students in the last two years have protested speech that they felt was offensive to them in a pro-speech manner."[16]

Is this quote from Porterfield a fair description of contemporary campus culture? Is free speech under attack at all—and if it is, are there any legal or administrative efforts to defend it or to organize and delineate permitted speech? Universities and colleges regularly rely on several tools to do so.

One possible tool is *an appeal to the First Amendment,* which famously protects speech in public contexts. It reads, "Congress shall make no law respecting an establishment of religion, or prohibiting the free exercise thereof; or abridging the freedom of speech, or of the press; or the right of the people peaceably to assemble, and to petition the Government for a redress of grievances."[17] Public institutions are clearly bound by the First Amendment, whereas private colleges and universities have more latitude in determining the kind of protections and exclusions that they permit on free speech—though private institutions, too, tend to abide by it, as well as by the general principles of academic freedom that apply to both faculty and students. Here is a relevant quote from the 1967 Joint Statement on Rights and Freedoms of Students, which has been endorsed by the American Association of University Professors, the Association of American Colleges and Universities, the National Student Association, and other organizations:

> Students bring to the campus a variety of interests previously acquired and develop many new interests as members of the academic community. They should be free to organize and join associations to promote their common interests. . . .
>
> Students and student organizations should be free to examine and discuss all questions of interest to them, and to express opinions publicly and privately. They should always be free to support causes by orderly means which do not disrupt the regular and essential operation of the institution. At the same time, it should be made clear to the academic and the larger community that in their public expressions or demonstrations students or student organizations speak only for themselves.[18]

It is clear from this statement as well as from events in recent years that the legal framework alone cannot do all the work required to protect free speech on campus or to respond to challenges and violations of this principle. The need for more specific principles regarding freedom in the context of university life has long been clear, giving rise both to statements like this one and to additional frameworks that organize and defend the freedoms of thought and action on campus.

While public universities are bound by the First Amendment and private universities often espouse versions of the same, free speech is not in fact a core value of the university. *Academic freedom* is a core value, and it does both more and less than free speech. Academic freedom is meant to protect researchers from political, institutional, and other pressures as they work to contribute to the advancement of knowledge. I will not enumerate here all the protections it provides but will focus for the purpose of the current discussion on main aspects relevant to speech protection. For instance, academic freedom is meant to protect free inquiry in the search for knowledge. The goal of the advancement of knowledge in certain ways limits free speech because it precludes in the context of research certain forms of speech—for example, it precludes plagiarism or mischaracterization of the results of research, even if those are protected by free speech norms. Still, academic freedom uses mechanisms like tenure to protect professors from being penalized for pursuing controversial lines of work and expressing unpopular views. (I discuss academic freedom in detail in chapter 4.)

The law prohibits or regulates various types of speech both on and off campus. Courts have recognized, for example, that harassment of one student by another can limit the harassed student's access to educational opportunities.[19] Other forms of speech that constitute threats or defamation can also be legally regulated and limited. In an attempt to clarify the boundaries that limit acceptable expression, some schools have adopted *speech codes* that list certain forms of speech that should be avoided on campus. Policies that forbid offensive speech, that list specific words or forms of expression that should not be used, and that limit protests and demonstrations to specific areas or times are all forms of speech codes. In recent years, "acceptable use" policies of technology platforms sometimes also include regulatory efforts to restrict expression online. Organizations dedicated to First Amendment protections see speech codes as infringements on free expression and academic exchange.[20] They are indeed best seen as such, and they are also rather ineffective as ways to deal with speech concerns on campus (as discussed in the next chapter).

These tools can pull in different directions, and clearly their implementation across different campuses in different eras has varied. Consider the arguments on both sides of the contentious cases briefly described above. Many have argued that the core mission of the university—namely, an open-minded search for truth and an equally open-minded climate for teaching—must be preserved at all costs. These critics have blasted student protestors from the University of Missouri to Yale for demanding adherence to strict, politically correct speech codes that limit competing or critical views. These commentators—who usually position themselves on the right and within libertarian circles but have found receptive audiences beyond these niches—reject concepts like safe spaces and trigger warnings, which are seen as efforts to protect students from perceived harms. In their view, research and teaching are badly compromised by the demand that free speech be curtailed for emotional reasons.

On the other side are those who worry that support for unchecked free speech can be used as a cover for promoting hateful views. Even if hate speech is protected by the First Amendment, they claim, it is still permissible for a campus to favor certain well-grounded, evidence-based, and open-minded views over others. It is reasonable for an educational institution to reject views that undermine the equality and dignity of some of its members, especially those who belong to racial, sexual, or other vulnerable minority groups. By this account, a commitment to free speech that does not account for the impact of voicing hurtful views on campus does not provide a reasonable response to the educational mission of the university, especially in an age of rising diversity. Protecting students and dismantling power relations that prioritize some views over others is arguably necessary for a democratic society to flourish. Some who adhere to this view suggest that free speech itself is a tool in maintaining unequal or undemocratic power structures.

To clarify why tensions between these views are not inevitable, and thus to pave the way for an inclusive freedom approach, let me start by dispelling three myths about free speech on campus.

**Myth #1: Free Speech Is a Concern
Only in Isolated Events on Campus**

Most of the public conversation about free speech on campus is focused on public events that erupt when a controversial speaker comes to campus. The attack on Charles Murray at Middlebury College, the protests and fires on Berkeley's campus that lead to the cancellation of Milo Yiannopoulos's event, the withdrawal of Condoleezza

Rice's invitation to serve as commencement speaker at Rutgers—all led to intense public scrutiny of the ways campuses handle speech. But speech, including controversial speech, is central to teaching and learning, and as such it is central to many aspects of campus life. It generates continuous disputes, tensions, and challenges on college campuses that only rarely become broader public controversies. Some of the most egregious attempts to limit free speech on campus today come not from within the liberal faction on campus but rather from state legislatures. Calls for outlawing BDS or Students for Justice in Palestine (groups opposing the Israeli occupation of the West Bank) and efforts to regulate what some legislatures see as liberal biases in coursework may be less visible than a Yiannopoulos talk, but they still threaten to limit freedom of association, thought, and expression by both students and instructors.

Even the intentional effort to inspire speech suppression and its attendant rage, which characterizes many of the clubs and groups that invite the likes of Yiannopoulos and Murray, usually ends with campus members expressing their distaste in agreeable ways and the event taking place as planned. The public nature of special events, especially ones that become exposed to public scrutiny after some dramatic flare-up, makes dealing with them more sensitive and difficult. However, those events, too, are best understood and dealt with in light of the overall approach the campus develops to the issue of free expression. There are many contexts beyond special events that should be considered just as central to a campus approach to free speech. A thoughtful approach to free speech on campus should incorporate considerations related to *classroom speech* (as discussed in chapter 4), *online communication* (as discussed in chapter 3), *student initiated events, and college/university initiated events*. It is a common error to assume that most events on campus are college-sponsored. As a result of this mistake, advocates both on and off campus regularly point to student-sponsored events and demand that the university or college prevent the event from taking place or otherwise take responsibility for it.

Allowing college administrators to oversee and regulate speech in these contexts would be unfortunate, as was clearly illustrated at Williams College when the president stepped in to cancel an event sponsored by a student group called "Uncomfortable Learning," which had invited a speaker widely considered to be racist.[21] It is easy to agree that the speaker in question is outside the political mainstream, and that some of his views, which he was invited to discuss, are racist. The student group that invited him (including its leader, who is African American) saw the invitation as an opportunity to engage with objectionable ideas in an open and conversational setting. The administration would have been wise to permit the event. If asked by alumni, its board of trustees, or the media about the matter, the college could have indicated that the views expressed by members of the community or by their invitees are never endorsed or even vetted by the college, as part of its commitment to free speech. However, in this case, Williams's president intervened because he judged the speaker's views to be "hate speech," not recognizing (or not accepting) that hate speech, too, is protected speech or that describing a view as hateful does not imply that the speech can, or should, be barred. In this case, the administration's intervention into a student group's event was unjustified.

The diffuse structures of colleges are central to the protection of free speech, as well as to the execution of various research and educational functions. A college or a university, as an administrative and public body, hardly ever invites or hosts speakers. Once a year, it invites commencement speaker(s) and hosts graduation ceremonies. There are rare other occasions, such as "university lectures," where a speaker is indeed hosted by the college or the university. But for the most part, it is a department, a student group, or another independent entity on campus that is responsible for an event.

This might sound immaterial or bureaucratic, but in fact the distinction is crucial to both understanding and preserving free speech. University and college central administrators—"The University" or "The College"—do not and should not control the communication, events, invitees, and exchanges that independent groups and departments within the college choose to hold. To give the institution or its administration the power to regulate events, speakers, and other forms of expression that departments and student groups currently hold is in effect to forgo free speech for the sake of administrative order.

Myth #2: Free Speech Controversies Should Be Resolved by Enforcing the Norms of Civility

In a recent survey, a majority of college and university provosts identified the decline in faculty civility as a concern in American higher education. The University of

Missouri's "Show Me Respect" project includes a "toolbox" that offers twenty ways to achieve civility.[22] It recommends acting in civil ways, offers rules about civility and ways to achieve it, and discusses the dire consequences of failing to do so—and it presents all of its tools as ways to prevent tensions surrounding controversial speech. As I make clear in chapters 3 and 4, the focus on civility is misguided: civility limits speech more than necessary, it can have a chilling effect, and it also tends to target forms of expression that are more likely to be used by individuals who feel harmed or excluded. Punishing these individuals for expressing their views does not support an open-minded and inclusive environment.

In his pained response to the violent protests against his talk at Middlebury, Charles Murray wrote, "We're talking about violations that involve a few hundred students, ranging from ones that call for a serious tutelary response . . . to ones calling for permanent expulsion (for the students who participated in the mob as we exited), to criminal prosecution (at the very least, for those who were physically violent) . . . I will urge . . . appropriate punishment in cases where the evidence is clear."[23] Punishment for violation of college honor codes and criminal or civil prosecutions are possible responses when things get out of hand at such events. But beyond the enforcement of the regular criminal code and basic codes of conduct at the college, making new rules or calling for tougher enforcement will most likely not resolve any of the issues that bring about these protests, as Murray recognizes in the same column. Calls for civility will not do the work either. There is no substitute for the ongoing commitment to a deliberate dialogue on the importance of free speech, to the protection of all individuals and groups (especially minority groups), and to the establishment and maintenance of a campus atmosphere where opinions can be debated openly and honestly.

All this is especially true when student speech is at stake. Academic freedom and tenure rules protect professors from suffering sanctions for what they say in class and for most of what they say outside of it as well—and for good reason. Punishing professors for expressing unpopular views would surely contribute to a chilling environment in which research cannot be pursued with an open mind for fear of retribution or punishment.[24] Students do not need the same type of protections, but they can benefit from knowing that they are free to try on different views and to engage in open debate and that they will be valued for their contributions rather than ridiculed, silenced, or punished. Speech protections require a general set of commitments and an open atmosphere on campus, along with general rules and guidelines. But speech controversies are rarely resolved by better enforcement or the addition of new civility rules, both of which risk creating an atmosphere in which freedom of speech and thought is discouraged.

Myth #3: You Need to Choose between Allowing Free Speech and Protecting Vulnerable Groups

Both those committed to pure free speech and those favoring the protection of vulnerable groups often assume that one needs to choose, that there is an inherent tension between the two principles. One side suggests that if we allow unfettered free speech, we'll end up with hateful and inciting speech that will harm, and maybe exclude, members of groups on campus; the other side assumes, meanwhile, that protecting members of these groups must necessarily require free speech to be strictly and unreasonably curtailed.

But in fact this tension can be alleviated by an ongoing, clear commitment by college leadership and members to create and sustain an environment conducive to open expression. While such an environment must operate within the boundaries of legal requirements, a more nuanced, responsive, and relational approach can often accomplish what a hundred regulations cannot. Any time (and especially in times of political and social tensions) a college can affirm in the broadest possible terms its commitment to the principle of free expression—and demonstrate its willingness to devote resources, including staff, to upholding this principle—the college should do so.

The following chapter develops a framework that cuts against the assumptions on both sides by showing how it's possible to promote both free speech and inclusion on campus.

Chapter 2

Inclusive Freedom

The events at Yale during Halloween 2015 started off with a letter from administrators encouraging sensitivity in costume choices, to which a lecturer, Erika Christakis, responded with an email in which she stated:

> I know that many decent people have proposed guidelines on Halloween costumes from a spirit of avoiding hurt and offense. I laud those goals, in theory, as most of us do. But in practice, I wonder if we should reflect more transparently, as a community, on the consequences of an institutional (bureaucratic and administrative) exercise of implied control over college students.
>
> I wonder, and I am not trying to be provocative: Is there no room anymore for a child or young person to be a little bit obnoxious . . . a little bit inappropriate or provocative or, yes, offensive? American universities were once a safe space not only for maturation but also for a certain regressive, or even transgressive,

experience; increasingly, it seems, they have become places of censure and prohibition. And the censure and prohibition come from above, not from yourselves! Are we all okay with this transfer of power? Have we lost faith in young people's capacity—in your capacity to exercise self-censure, through social norming, and also in your capacity to ignore or reject things that trouble you?

Christakis lived on campus along with her husband, Nicholas Christakis, a professor. In response to her e-mail, a group of students rallied together to try to have them both removed. In an emotionally charged meeting with Nicholas, students argued that it was his role, as a residential master, not to foster intellectual debate and difficult conversations but rather to create and protect a safe space—a "home" environment—for students.[1]

Protests continued on campus in the following weeks, and Yale's president released a new set of campus initiatives, including recruiting a more diverse faculty and expanding institutional support at campus cultural centers. In addition, Nicholas took a year's sabbatical and stepped down from his residential role, while Erika resigned. In an e-mail to the *Washington Post* after her resignation, she wrote, "I worry that the current climate at Yale is not, in my view, conducive to the civil dialogue and open inquiry required to solve our urgent societal problems."[2]

Erika Christakis was probably right. Civil dialogue is hard to sustain when many feel that they are not equal parties to the dialogue and when the overall atmosphere on campus is not open to dissenting views. While Yale may be in a particularly precarious situation in this regard with its perennial controversies over speech,[3] it seems that speech on college campuses has become embroiled in the current culture wars in the United States. The left is often worried about rampant hate being protected by appeals to free speech, while the right voices concerns about liberal professors limiting expression and indoctrinating students in the name of inclusion and diversity. Thoughtful commentators—and I see Erika Christakis as one—get caught in the middle of this polarized debate. This alone is a reason to rethink the positions expressed today about free speech and to seek a more productive way to reframe the debate, ideally in a less polarizing way. But there are other reasons to focus on free speech on campus specifically, as part of a broader conversation about democracy. Campus free speech deserves its own place within the debate on free speech because of the role that universities and colleges serve in society, because of the population they serve, and also because of some shifts in the social function of campuses.

Colleges and universities are places where knowledge is developed and disseminated. To do their job well, scholars and students require the freedom to inquire, question, and probe established views and new visions without fear of retribution or silencing. The freedom to explore, to express and consider controversial views, and to raise remote options and pursue them is central to research, teaching, and learning. Free speech protections are therefore necessary if researchers and their students are to make the kinds of contributions that society expects them to make, and for which they come to campus in the first place.

In addition, the biggest constituency on campus is young adults, newly minted as full citizens but often not fully prepared for their civic roles.[4] While some campuses focus more on research and the generation of knowledge and others focus more on their educational mission, all residential campuses are charged with supervising and supporting the young adults in their charge. It should be expected as a matter of course that large groups of young people would try on their new status by crossing various boundaries, more and less productively. Underage drinking is by no means the only way in which they test their new independence, and the development and testing of new ideas, views, and beliefs is indeed a more common, and more acceptable, expression of budding adulthood.

Moreover, for many students, campus is the most diverse community they have encountered so far in their young lives. Families, neighborhoods, schools, and places of worship tend to be cohesive and relatively mono-chromatic, either by their very nature and mission or as a result of long processes of social separation. Thus for instance, public schools—despite being seen by many of their advocates and by the families who benefit from them as microcosms of the public—are increasingly segregated by race and class.[5] Students' new campus community, often more diverse than others they have lived in—even if not as diverse as it aspires to be—invites them to consider their own often unquestioned beliefs, views, and forms of expression as they relate to other individuals and groups.

Colleges now serve a larger number of students from more diverse backgrounds than ever before, and therefore should both respond to their various needs and build on the interests and knowledge that they bring to campus.[6]

The makeup of the campus student body (and staff) should inform the processes of protecting and encouraging speech. Free speech on campus requires a reassessment today not only because of significant changes in the diversity and levels of polarization in American society but also because of how those are reflected on campus. People from a wider array of backgrounds pursue degrees that are now requirements for many careers and predictors of civic participation. Racial diversity among college students has increased, and African Americans' share of undergraduate students now just about reflects their share in society, as it grew from 10 percent in 1976 to 14 percent in 2012. Hispanic enrollment rose from 3 to 14 percent in the last three decades.[7] A growing number of international students attend American colleges, adding their own interests, needs, and political views into the mix.

Why would changes in demographic makeup require that we rethink the way we delineate and protect free speech? Decades ago, when newly admitted or promoted women on some campuses called for the expansion of the canon to include works and perspectives by women, their point was not just that excluding women authors from syllabi was harmful or offensive (though it surely reflected bias) but also that it reflected laziness of thought and resulted in poor quality research and teaching. Assuming that the university could simply add women without any curricular changes ignored how the university's mission was advanced by widening perspectives. Expectations about campus relations needed—and still need—to change. Women rightly claim, for example, that harassment should not be seen as an inevitable or natural aspect of workplace and teaching relations but rather should be recognized as a form of discrimination that bars (usually) women from access to learning.

Today, the diversity of the campus community is not merely a result of changing demographics in the country, but in fact reflects an expansion of the university's social mission. While maintaining its commitment to research and inquiry, the university has grown from an institution that serves a small segment of the population deemed eligible to become religious, political, economic, and thought leaders to one that serves as an engine for social mobility and equal opportunity. Contemporary demands that high schools prepare all students to be "career and college ready," a graduation rate that now possibly exceeds 80 percent, and the diverse pool of applicants creates changes well beyond the admissions office. The evolving makeup of the community on campus requires attention to the ways in which members of groups that were excluded either formally or effectively in the past are incorporated into campus. Such incorporation must go well beyond the attention given at the admissions office (in light of evolving Supreme Court and state court rulings on the matter) to gender, race, income level, and other attributes and indicators. It should also take into account the responsiveness of the campus to the needs of these relatively new populations, such as support for first-generation students and cultural student organizations. Many colleges are learning to recognize that a part of the attention that needs to be paid to a diverse student body relates to speech and expression. The needed changes include rethinking the ways diverse views, perspectives, and expressions are welcomed and responded to.

Of course, not all campuses are home to similarly diverse student bodies. Some colleges are open only to women. Historically black colleges and universities are open to all but serve a student population that mostly identifies as African American. Some local and regional colleges are located in geographical areas that are home to mostly one ethnic or racial group, and their student bodies are relatively homogeneous. Some campuses serve "blue" or "red" parts of the United States, and their student populations reflect the ideological inclinations of their region. Some other forms of diversity are less evident but not less important: in some colleges, most students come from affluent households, making first-generation and low-income students a small and sometimes marginalized group; in other colleges, the majority of students are the first in their families to go to college, and many struggle with financial concerns. The opportunity that many college campuses provide to sexual minorities to live openly, as evidenced by the welcome proliferation of relevant student groups and public statements like those in the "It Gets Better" campaign, adds another dimension of expressed diversity to campus. On many campuses, nontraditional students—those who start their studies at a later age than usual—are attending in growing numbers. Since campus demographics affect the type of speech issues the campus deals with—because speech reflects the relationship on campus, and those change with the makeup of the student body, among other things—these differences across different campus communities are significant for the discussion of speech on campus.

While the actual tensions that arise as a result of the demographic makeup of the student body are significant, two other points also should be kept in mind. First, all campuses are diverse in some way. However, ideology, class background, citizenship status, sexual orientation, and other parameters are not always seen, and with a sense of homogeneity, students who are different might feel compelled to "pass"—to hide their true identities as gay, conservative, Muslim, or undocumented—to avoid the tensions that may arise from an evident minority status. Some young adults might still look to fit in. It is important to create an environment in which students do not find it necessary to hide their identities, because of the harm to their well-being as well as the resultant loss of a valuable opportunity for peers to challenge their own views and to engage with a diverse set of perspectives that they may not have considered.

Second, even a campus community that is relatively homogeneous by some measures and calm in terms of the relational issues that give rise to free speech concerns still resides within the same diverse, polarized country. While the campus may serve as respite or "safe space" for those who come there to study and socialize, part of the campus mission is still to challenge students, to make them think, to expand their intellectual horizons, and to prepare them for their civic roles. To do so, the campus needs to expose students to some of the tensions and disagreements that they might encounter outside of the bubble created by a homogeneous campus social environment. The leadership on campus, as well as some of the faculty, may recoil from this suggestion, fearing the possibility of raising tensions where none exist. Clearly there is no need to generate artificial tensions or clashes, but students deserve the opportunity to grow and expand their perspectives. Preserving a false sense of security that comes from never having one's views challenged or encountering diverse peers (or faculty) limits the benefits that college should provide. Addressing issues of speech and expression requires a framework that is aimed at protecting free speech for all members of the campus community in ways that support the development of an inclusive environment.

An inclusive freedom framework for speech on campus takes seriously the importance of a free and open exchange as a necessary condition for the pursuit of knowledge and as a contributing condition to the development of civic and democratic capacities. It lends similar weight to the related demand that all members of the campus community be able to participate in this free and open exchange if it is to accomplish the goals of free inquiry, open-minded research, and equal access to learning and to civic development.

A call for creating an inclusive environment in which all members are respected and where all voices can be heard should be framed and recognized as furthering rather than impeding the realization of a free and open campus. Students sometimes call on campus administrators to support inclusion and diversity by limiting speech,[8] and they refer to harms caused to them by instances in which open expression allows for hurtful speech to take center stage. But an inclusive and welcoming campus is one that must recognize the necessity of free speech.

To see how inclusion and free speech can coincide rather than stand in opposition, a closer look is needed at what "harm" means in the context of the free speech cases discussed here. In order to bridge the divide between those who seek to protect speech from attacks by advocates of inclusion and those who seek to protect minority groups from attacks by proponents of free speech, we need to clarify what is the harm that the latter are aiming to avoid.

The notion of harm has been central to the liberal debate at least since it was articulated by John Stuart Mill, who famously noted that "the only purpose for which power can be rightfully exercised over any member of a civilized community, against his will, is to prevent harm to others."[9] Harm to others is thus to him the only justified reason to limit the freedom of any member in a democratic community, although Mill is sometimes understood to have claimed that you still have a right to speak even if your words harm others.[10] As articulated after the Middlebury events by Cornel West and Robert P. George, two eminent scholars who represent opposing ideological views, "All of us should be willing—even eager—to engage with anyone who is prepared to do business in the currency of truth-seeking discourse by offering reasons, marshaling evidence, and making arguments."[11] By this view, very few instances of speech can constitute harm, if harm even remains a relevant aspect of the debate. There are cases for limiting free speech in the name of preventing harm to others—yelling "fire" in a crowded theater and publicizing libelous statements about another person are famous examples. But for the most part, when views and opinions are expressed as part of an open, democratic exchange, they should be permissible.

However, this expansive view of free speech as rarely causing harm and therefore usually not being subject to censure can reasonably be put into question in the context of the diversifying campus. Harmful speech is discussed in more detail in the next chapter in the context of identity politics on campus. For now, it will suffice to clarify: recognizing that some forms of speech are harmful and that these harms compound other (historical and current) harms does not mean that speech should be more commonly censored or curtailed. Rather, attention to speech is called for by issues surrounding it, such as the possible motivations of speakers, including "the troll problem"—speakers who intend merely to be provocative rather than to inform, challenge, or generate dialogue.[12] In addition, the possible impact of words can be part of the consideration, both immediately and in the aggregate accumulation of small harms. Again, while the response should not be to shut down or avoid speech, additional steps can reasonably be taken by other student groups and sometimes even by the campus leadership. Forms of expression (and behavior) that were seen as mainstream when the campus was all-male, all-white, or presumed to be all-straight—such as using casual sexist, racist, and antigay language—are being challenged by some as preventing members of newer groups from being recognized as full members of the campus community.

Advocates' calls to give "no platform" to such speakers miss the mark because they seek to avoid perspectives that deserve or, at the very least, require dialogue—if some or many in society hold certain views, even reprehensible ones, avoiding them does nothing to challenge them. For liberals of different races who hold clear views on racial equality, for example, speaking to Charles Murray would surely provide an opportunity to challenge his views without risking their own intellectual integrity or sense of self-worth. Shortly after the events at Middlebury, Murray was scheduled to speak at the invitation of a professor at Notre

Dame, who wrote, "Notre Dame is one of Charles Murray's first post-Middlebury campus lectures. It makes our event a referendum on free speech and how universities handle controversial speakers. I didn't intend for his visit to address these issues, but it now does. Given the trends of cancelled lectures, ever-increasing calls to disinvite speakers, and ideological bullying on college campuses, we must take a stand for civil discourse and reasoned engagement. We must show that universities can host respectful conversations among people who disagree."[13] But clearly intellectual exchange is not the focus for everyone. Rather, progressive activists are concerned that voicing what they perceive—possibly correctly—as racially charged or even racist views would harm members of racial minority groups on campus and therefore should be silenced. For them, standing for civil discourse and reasoned engagement, and even more so the commitment to respectful conversation, requires that speakers respect all their audience members, a stance that misogyny, homophobia, and racism preclude.

Like the Yale case, which started off with advice against donning hurtful costumes, many speech cases in recent years have been framed as issues related to causing and avoiding harm or searching for safety in the face of potential or actual harm. For opponents of this view, the demand to avoid harm is tantamount to an attack on a core value of the university, as outlined in the 2016 letter to freshmen from the University of Chicago, which declared that safe spaces and trigger warnings would not be provided. But in fact the collective effort to avoid harm is an important step in constructing a free and equal community of inquiry, which is the shared goal in this debate, and should thus be taken seriously by those on both sides of the free speech divide.

In response to the attack on Charles Murray at Middlebury, its student government association issued a statement recommending that departments and student organizations "respect the boundaries of the College's community standards . . . in order to create a better learning environment."[14] This line of response is typical to the frame of mind that sees free speech mostly through the lens of offense and that presumes an inherent tension between protecting free expression and protecting vulnerable groups from (further) harm. Some progressives and liberals have come to fear that, by hosting speakers like Murray, conservative student groups are invoking free speech to cover up an insidious attempt to promote hate-based and evidence-free speech and to incite anger rather than to create a meaningful opportunity for learning and dialogue. This is a reasonable concern in the context of an educational institution, but nonetheless it should not be used to curtail free speech. Curtailing free speech based on content or—even worse—the presumed motivation of the speaker, raises the risk of creating some version of thought police—namely, a regulatory mechanism for deciding which views and opinions warrant an invitation to campus and which do not. This is not to say that there is no space for response, and some options are suggested below, but it does mean that the liberal concern about hate-based and evidence-free or inciting events, even if justified, should not result in a call for censoring or curtailing events and speakers.

Polarized views on free speech produced the Chicago "no trigger warnings here" letter, assuming that if professors provide trigger warnings as a way to protect vulnerable students from potential harm, they will be compromising their commitment to open-minded research and the spirit and principles of free expression. On the other side, they produced the call from Middlebury students "to articulate some parameters for which viewpoints are worthy" of the process of free inquiry,[15] asserting that a stricter limitation on permissible speech on campus would give rise to a more inclusive community.

This perceived tension is mostly misguided, and the framework that presumes an opposition between free inquiry on the one hand and inclusion on the other juxtaposes views that could potentially overlap through a shared commitment to protect free and inclusive speech. The presumed tension between free speech and protection from harm is the result of a rigid and inaccurate description of both, and a charitable and close reading of the above statements that articulate both sides shows a commitment to similar values. The University of Chicago seemed to be blindsided by the backlash to their letter, and in response they took pains to clarify their commitment to an open and equitable campus where all are welcome and respected. The Middlebury students who circulated the "Broken Inquiry" statement after the Murray event expressed a sense of dismay at his invitation and perspective, but they still articulated as their first principle the view that "genuine higher learning is possible only where free, reasoned, and civil speech and discussion are respected."[16] There seems to be an agreement—even if thin, even if only as lip service—that free speech and inquiry are central tenets of university or college life and its mission, and that diversity, equity, and inclusion need to be respected. Not often enough is it acknowledged that equity and inclusion do not have to stand in the way of free speech and open-minded inquiry and that the two can go hand in hand in promoting the key mission of higher education institutions.

Moreover, both sides fail to take account of how their views can readily become self-defeating. When social justice advocates call for the curtailment of free speech through censoring speakers and canceling events, they neglect to recognize the historical reality that curtailing free speech might harm vulnerable groups. Once censorship based on content is possible, what is to stop people in power—administrators, religious majority groups, or other established centers of power—from limiting speech by dissenters, opponents, or anyone who threatens the status quo?

On the other hand, free speech advocates who insist that unfettered free speech is a necessary condition for the open-minded free inquiry that makes a university worth its name sidestep the fact that when many on campus are effectively silenced, inquiry is in fact neither free nor open-minded. It remains the prerogative of those who have the tools and support to join the conversation and to participate in the main activities on campus, including research, active learning, and established social roles. Many women, racial and sexual minorities, first-generation students, and other individuals who may not see themselves (or be seen by others) as belonging or possess the tools required to hit the ground running remain outside the conversation, impoverishing the conversation and hindering the search for truth and knowledge.

It is commonly said that the only cure for inaccurate or even harmful speech is more and better speech.[17] Inclusive freedom is aligned with this stance in one sense: colleges should not aim to enforce civility or regulate speech but should focus, rather, on providing ample opportunities for students to develop and express their views, question, and even rebel. Curtailing speech to prevent controversy is both unjustified and ineffective; instead, colleges should aim to enable multiple forms of expressive and political speech, guided by no more than broad legal requirements and a thin, flexible commitment to an inclusive atmosphere. The latter should be used not to limit speech but to support students in developing opportunities for further speech and the capacity to productively respond to speech that they find offensive rather than to look for ways to shut it down.

However, this does not mean that colleges should not develop and enforce practices meant to ensure that all can express their views. The University of Chicago report aims to do just that by calling for "consistency across cases" and developing "procedures for event management to reduce the chances that those engaged in disruptive conduct can prevent others from speaking or being heard."[18] But their focus on disciplinary measures is insufficient and hence regrettable. While students who are acting in inappropriately disruptive ways or preventing speakers from being heard may suffer disciplinary consequences if they fail to act in accordance with the general expectation, couching free speech practices in the context of disciplinary measures is unproductive because the main issues are civic, relational, and educational rather than regulatory.

Along with changes in demographics, the university's mission has changed from the early days of focusing on leadership preparation to the current emphasis on professional and civic development. A diverse campus requires changes to syllabi, in classroom practices and activities, and in attitudes around campus to reflect broader visions and to provide all members of the campus community with opportunities to learn and work. Listening and responding to these demands can promote the revised social mission of the university—serving a diverse population alongside pursuing truth through honest and open-minded research and teaching. The two are best understood as reinforcing each other rather than standing in tension to each other (though tensions can arise in specific cases). If pedagogy and other campus practices are not expanded in response to a changing student body, many students will feel and be shut out of participating in learning and other activities, which not only is hurtful but also represents a failure to consider new and important forms of experience and knowledge. The suppression of views that occurs when diverse students are not provided with full access to learning and other benefits that the campus offers not only is a social harm but represents a blind side in the search for knowledge. It thus serves as a limitation on the college's effort to fulfill its research mission and to disseminate knowledge, in addition to indicating a lack of respect.

Increasingly diverse campus communities raise challenges that have recently included demands to change building names and calls to create more inclusive and sensitive social environments in contexts such as holiday celebrations, dining hall menus, and Greek parties to name a few. Some of these issues are being framed as demands for safe spaces that would provide students with protection from harm to their well-being, identity, and sense of security, as well as with an affirmation of their belonging.

The next two chapters envision the ways to implement inclusive freedom on campus in light of these challenges—first on the quad (meaning in the public, social, and extracurricular context of campus activities) and then in the classroom.

Identity and Free Speech on the Quad

In recent years, controversies surrounding free speech have increasingly involved issues of identity, with left-leaning groups leading efforts to curb speech they see as harmful, particularly to the equal standing of marginalized groups. It has become more acceptable relative to previous eras for a student or another member of the campus community to point to harm caused by speech directed to members of a particular identity group, such as sexual, racial, or religious minorities, and to demand that this speech be censored or the speaker punished. In this chapter, I discuss the place of identity politics in the debate surrounding speech on campus and suggest that while identity should be recognized and sometimes protected as a platform for affiliation and expression on campus, it should not serve as justification for imposing limitations on open expression. Moreover, students should be encouraged to not rely solely or mainly on identity groups for political expression; rather, they should be invited to learn to extend their sense of themselves as political actors beyond their identity groups. Colleges should fulfill their civic and educational missions by protecting and encouraging political and other forms of speech by individual students and student groups. Students should not be perceived or encouraged to act in ways that insulate them from conflicting views; exposure to opposition and disagreement should not be included in the notion of harm from which students must be protected.

In 1936, University of Chicago chancellor Robert Maynard Hutchins wrote that a liberal education frees a person "from the prison-house of his class, race, time, place, background, family, and even his nation."[1] Today many progressives would insist that such freedom is neither feasible nor a desirable aspiration. The demand that students learn to shed their particular identities as they gain an education is not only impossible to fulfill; it is also seen today as discriminatory. Presumably, what remains after we shed our specific attributes is a shared rational mind, which many see as a product of Western, male, white thinking—one that rejects insights from other genders, cultures, or perspectives. A good education can allow individuals to overcome the tenets of their upbringing and identity or affirm them, but it does not require students to shed their attachments or sense of place. A good educational atmosphere allows room for identities and group-based visions as part of an open and inclusive environment and provides all members opportunities to navigate these possibilities and their own evolving commitments. This atmosphere is better than impoverishing our conversation by shedding all experiences, bodies, and differences in order to include all individuals in a homogeneous way, and it allows the campus conversation to be enriched by all views rather than pretending to coalesce around a shared vision.

Students must be permitted to organize with their peers if they are to have the power to express their views within the college's administrative and social structures. Freedom of association is a necessary condition for protecting free speech and maintaining an environment of open expression. Hence "safe spaces" where students can associate with those who are "like them"—racially, ideologically, or by any other measure—should be fully permissible, even as the university overall maintains its commitment to intellectual candor and to introducing controversial and uncomfortable ideas. Safe spaces and challenging ideas are not and should not be considered mutually exclusive.[2]

Many progressive and liberal-leaning members of campus communities are committed to protecting members of vulnerable and marginalized groups from violation of their rights. Some have come to see the protection of free speech as a tool for preserving the status quo, allowing the majority and those in power to express offensive and derogatory views without repercussions under the guise of protected speech. Often they voice concern both about the protection of overt racism or sexism and about "microaggressions"—the insidious, daily onslaught of indignities that individuals suffer because of their identities (e.g., as women, queer people, racial or ethnic minorities).

In recent years, political ideology itself has turned more and more into an aspect of one's identity in society, and even more so among young identity-conscious students. Clearly, one's political ideology may not be an aspect of one's identity in the same way that race, gender, or sexuality is, but for many it is still a significant source of identification, connection, and action. Political ideology is generally more a matter of choice than most aspects of one's identity, even as there are aspects of choice in many others. I use the loose metaphor of ideology as identity to indicate that for some, particularly young people and especially in our era of political polarization, their political commitments encompass much of who they are, what they stand for, their aspirations, and with whom they affiliate.

In a time of polarized public debate, political and ideological standpoints can feel like a mark of identity rather than a mere perspective or position. Therefore, one can readily be criticized for not properly falling in line with the views required of members of their ideological tribe; denying the reasonableness, good intentions, or even the humanity of members of the other tribe can readily follow.[3]

Providing and protecting opportunities for students to express their affiliations and identities without recrimination or humiliation are part of the commitment to inclusive freedom, but sometimes freedom of expression seems to run counter to the protection of marginalized identity groups, as was the case recently at Middlebury College.

The Middlebury Case

Author Charles Murray was invited to Middlebury College in early 2017 by the Middlebury Enterprise Club to speak about his recent book *Coming Apart*. Notorious for his 1994 book, *The Bell Curve*, Murray has been widely criticized for his supposedly racist views, which he denies, and for other aspects of his earlier work. Prior to the event, 450 alumni signed a letter that described the college's decision to host Murray as "unacceptable and unethical."[4] The authors of the letter demanded that the college disinvite Murray on the grounds that the college should not provide a platform for a hateful speech that would be based on work that is both methodologically suspect (as it has been described by many of Murray's peers) and marred by pseudoscientific justifications of racial hierarchy. The event, which did end up taking place, culminated in a violent encounter between angry protestors and the speaker and his entourage, with the host of the event suffering an injury.

Some fights over the invitation of certain speakers are political in the traditional sense. When students (and others) interrupted a talk by former CIA director John Brennan on the University of Pennsylvania's campus in 2016, they were expressing objections to the wars in which he had participated as a leader, and especially to drone strikes.[5] Chinese students at University of California, San Diego—another relatively new group of students in American campuses—objected to the invitation of the Dalai Lama as commencement speaker in 2017. These are political perspectives that are voiced in the public sphere. Although sometimes they go beyond what is acceptable on campus, as the protesters against Brennan did when they shut down his talk, political action and expressing political visions, including fringe ones, should be seen as part of campus and public life.

Other positions taken by students are tied more to the goals of protecting specific populations from harm.

Demands for safety and protection, including calls for the establishment of safe spaces, are bound up with identity politics and with the specific ways in which individuals learn to understand themselves as members of different groups. Calls for safe spaces are phrased in group identity terms, commonly demanding that students who belong to historically and currently marginalized groups—such as LGBT+ students, African Americans, women, immigrants, and religious minorities—be protected from structural, intentional, and casual forms of oppression. The Middlebury confrontation falls into this class of demands.

When responding to demands for safety or for suppressing speech in the name of inclusivity, campus administrators, faculty, and student groups should not focus solely on students' needs and should not automatically move to support or protect them. Overall, students are not asking their peers, faculty, and administration only for sensitive consideration, and they are not for the most part presenting themselves solely or mostly as vulnerable (though they are commonly portrayed as such). While members of historically marginalized or currently vulnerable populations sometimes need protection from physical and verbal aggression, they are more commonly looking for a space where their voices can be heard and their identities or visions properly represented, affirmed, and expressed.

As one of the Middlebury protesters noted after the event:

> The choice appeared stark: I could either protect Murray's academic freedom and our college's commitment to intellectual debate, or I could stand up

for those students—black, Latino, female, and lower income—whom Murray, in his book *The Bell Curve*, claimed are in an unequal position in society seemingly because of their genetic inferiority. I feared . . . I would become what the Rev. Dr. Martin Luther King Jr. called the "white moderate" in his "Letter from Birmingham Jail," someone who "is more devoted to 'order' than justice." . . . But as the protests continued, and Murray stayed silenced, I grew more and more concerned . . . am I also resisting intellectually open inquiry?[6]

Portraying the protesting students as vulnerable or refusing to think seems simplistic and unfair. Their rejection of Murray's views (again, putting aside the violence, which deserves to be condemned) is an effort to expand the democratic reach of free speech to groups they see as harmed and silenced, not an effort to protect themselves within a liberal cocoon.

Sometimes demands for safe spaces are calls for a place of respite. The student at Yale who was recorded shouting in frustration at Nicholas Christakis, claiming that she needs to feel at home, was widely derided, but her request is valid within the limited boundaries of college housing and other associational contexts. Some students may want to feel close to their peers, and that sometimes allows identity-based associations as part of the wider network of relations on campus. Clubs, dorms, and other social environments that permit differentiation by gender (e.g., single-sex dorms), religion (e.g., associations on campus and houses of worship), or political ideology (e.g., College Republicans or Democrats, Enterprise Clubs, Students for Choice) are all permissible and in fact desirable aspects of campus and public life. They allow students to develop relationships with others who are like them in various ways and to reach out beyond their identity groups with the sense of confidence and connection that a place of respite can offer.

But at other times, calls for safe spaces should be reframed as calls for recognition of one's contribution to a conversation taking place in a diverse context. Defending his university's position in its letter to freshmen in 2016, University of Chicago president Robert Zimmer gave an interview to *The Wall Street Journal* to clarify the university's rejection of safe spaces. He explained:

> The main thing one always needs to keep in mind to contextualize all of these issues is the overarching purpose of universities. The purpose is to be a place that gives the most empowering education to students and creates an environment for the most imaginative and challenging work of faculty. Confrontation of multiple ideas and ideas that are different from one's own is critical to this. I think it's very important not to allow universities to slip into an environment in which they are allowing a kind of suppression of speech, or are allowing discomfort with different ideas to create a chilled environment for discourse.[7]

Per this view, safe spaces are equated with comfort, and this comfort is seen as standing in direct opposition to "empowering education" and "confrontation of multiple ideas." To the extent that the demand for safety is a demand for intellectual and social apathy, there is clearly no reason to defend it. But dismissing students' calls for safety as resulting from a narrow-minded pursuit of comfort or as an attempt to avoid the challenging work of confronting new ideas and reconsidering one's beliefs seems in itself to be narrow-minded and an expression of a refusal to listen not only to students' needs but also to their intellectual demands.

Current Chicago undergraduates, both liberal and conservative, expressed dismay at the letter on a similar basis. One argued that while students should indeed develop critical thinking, they "should not expect to have their life experiences belittled." Another wrote that the mere format and formality of an open discussion does not mean that all students are respected or heard in the same way: "Imagine a core social-science seminar in which the conversation turns to police brutality and racial bias. If the class consists of 20 students and reflects the racial composition of the college, one or two of them will be black. If these students' attitudes towards police brutality reflect national averages, the black students will see a connection between police brutality and racial bias while a majority of their classmates won't."[8]

If the culture on campus and in class is such that these two students feel uncomfortable expressing their views, not only are they harmed by feeling excluded and having their speech suppressed, but the class as a whole misses important and prevalent perspectives that remain unspoken. The call for providing students with safe spaces and other identity-related accommodations or protections cannot be dismissed as a liberal effort to avoid confronting other views, nor is it right to ridicule it as the response of overly protected "crybullies." In many cases, as illustrated here, students are not retreating to the safety of their unchecked beliefs, but rather they are challenging the orthodoxies of free speech and identity by demanding that free expression be made available to all, including many who have traditionally been silenced and too often still are. Moreover, they are rightly demanding not just that free speech is extended as a matter of formality—clearly no one was telling the two students not to speak their minds—but that it is provided effectively and practically as a matter of campus culture.

Identity and Harmful Speech

The experiences of students of different backgrounds on campus call for attention to the ways in which identity can hamper speech as well as to the ways in which speech can harm students based on their identities. Where do we draw the line between acceptable and unacceptable speech? Do legal lines suffice (such as those forbidding libel or threats)? Must the campus also prevent exclusion or harm, and how will the two be differentiated? How do we bridge the distance between what is legally permissible and what is socially harmful and exclusionary to some (while seeming to others to be a simple attempt to present legitimate views or challenge orthodox or entrenched visions)?

Inclusive freedom demands that speech on campus be protected as broadly as possible while aiming to ensure that all members of the campus community are recognized—and know that they are recognized—as members in good standing.

This aim becomes harder to realize when instructors, speakers, and students express views that some members of the community see as undermining their basic dignity, casting them as less than full members. The harm to some members' dignity is sometimes seen as reason enough to limit speech, as was clear in the Middlebury case. Charles Murray's very presence on campus, even if to speak about matters unrelated to *The Bell Curve*, was seen as undermining the dignity of African-American students, robbing them of their standing as full and equal members of the campus community. Harm to dignity has been framed by some legal scholars as reason to limit speech in certain contexts (like a campus) or even legally regulate the permissibility of making certain statements that can cause dignitary harms. Jeremy Waldron argues that when legally protected speech constitutes an assault on human dignity, it can and should be regulated to avoid this harm.[9] This framing draws attention away from the common focus on the speaker's autonomy and liberty, which many agree should be protected, and instead focuses on the impact of his speech on vulnerable members of the community. The concern then is not so much about the speaker and whether she is allowed to express herself but about the dignity of certain members of her potential audience or on their ability to be seen and to operate as equal members of the community. Because speech is not merely expressive but can also "be designed to wound, terrify, discourage, and dismay,"[10] Waldron and others have suggested that it should be permissible in a democratic context to regulate such speech so as to avoid undermining the dignity of those who hear the speech.

Moreover, when speakers make an argument that undermines the dignity of an individual or when they proclaim that members of a certain group of people are less valuable than others, less capable than others, or generally less than fully equal, it would be a mistake to focus only on the fact that the speakers were probably within their rights to make these statements. The context in which the statements take place matters, and the impact of the words should also be considered, especially in an educational institution and where the potential harm would be done to young people. For Waldron and others, the harmful effect of hate speech—the fact, which is hard to deny, that speech that causes dignitary harm can silence members of already vulnerable groups and put their equal status as members of the community into question—is reason enough to regulate that speech or even to ban it. There are strong arguments on this side, especially because the notion of free speech requires that all are able to speak, and if some individuals or groups are effectively discouraged from speaking, the environment created is not one of open-minded inquiry and debate. Inclusive freedom on campus, however, recognizes these harms and seeks to address them in other ways that are suitable for educational institutions while refraining from regulating and censoring speech based on its content.

To address these harms to dignity, it is necessary to recognize that they are not randomly distributed. The individuals and groups that are harmed, that see their equal standing in the community undermined, are already vulnerable and their status as equal members of the community in question is oftentimes newer and not always broadly accepted. When Milo Yiannopoulos makes fun of a transgender student in a public speech at the university that this student attends, he is not picking on any random person in the audience; rather, he is making a point about political correctness or the limits on allowable speech at the expense of a person who is already vulnerable and whose status as an equal member is already put into question by some. When Charles Murray questions the intellectual capacities of African Americans, he is offering a scientific-sounding rationale to biases and discriminatory tendencies and perceptions that already exist in society. Speaking about the supposed genetic explanation for African American underperformance on tests (and ignoring plausible alternative explanations, such as social factors like stereotype threats[11] or the limitations of the tests themselves) sounds to many less like a disinterested discussion of a scientific hypothesis than an insult and a dignitary harm. When Lawrence Summers suggested that women might have a lower aptitude in math and science as one possible reason for women's underrepresentation at the top of some science fields, this comment was received not—as he claims that it was intended—as one possible hypothesis among others but rather as the president of Harvard proposing that women are not smart enough to excel in math and science.

The problem, then, is not so much the anecdotal or local harmful effect of speech but rather its accumulating and insidious effect. Harmful speech of this type compounds the silencing of certain groups by designating them as less than equal members of the community. As Miranda Fricker has argued, views and opinions are oftentimes assessed ad hominem, based on the speaker rather than the content of speech.[12] The harm is embedded in the assumption that some people cannot participate in the conversation at the same level of knowledge, meaning they and their views are not equally valued. The demands of civility are founded on the assumptions that we can all calmly and respectfully voice our opinions and listen to others' views, that we can weigh the different perspectives offered in the conversation using a shared metric, and that all views will be assessed on their merits. But when a participant in a debate is not recognized as an equal, he can find himself in a vicious cycle—the more he tries to assert his view, the more unreasonable he will seem to any participants predisposed to suspect his capacity to engage reasonably in the first place. This is what Fricker calls "epistemic injustice"—the injustice that occurs when knowledge and perspective are not recognized as valid because the identity of the speaker as a knower is put into question.

The threat of harm, including harm to the dignity of already vulnerable individuals and groups, should be recognized and accounted for. But what kind of response should it generate? For Waldron, this type of harm merits a legislative response, one that would criminalize or otherwise regulate speech that undermines dignity in this way. He sees this type of harmful expression and hate speech as "group libel" or "group defamation," which can reasonably be regulated in similar legal ways to those we use to regulate personal libel or defamation. Many scholars, as well as the American Civil Liberties Union, question this conclusion and argue that its legal grounding is insufficient. Inclusive freedom on campus would require recognizing the harms Waldron discusses and developing ways to address them other than those he suggests.

Sensitivity to inclusion in all its forms should not be enacted through an attack on freedom; it should not be pursued as a matter of course by calling for limits on freedom of speech. Progressives and others who are committed to equality for all members of the community and to protecting members of vulnerable groups (which can at different times include women, sexual and gender minorities, or religious, racial, and ethnic minorities) sometimes call for limiting specific expression based on its misogynic, racist, or anti-LGBT+ content.[13] Limiting permissible speech to strengthen inclusion does little to protect minority groups. Censorship of legally protected speech is harmful not only to democratic ideals but also to the minority groups that the censorship seeks to protect. Once censorship based on viewpoint becomes part of the campus procedures and regulations, there is no guarantee that it will stop with the specific perspectives it was introduced to block. Equivalencies, including false ones, are bound to be introduced into the procedure either by administrators seeking a sense of balance or by student groups with competing views ("If we protect black students, we need to also protect white students" or "If antigay speech is blocked because it is offensive to the LGBT+ community, we need to also consider the feelings of religious students who view homosexuality as a sin"). Silencing offensive speech is also too limited a tool, focusing on the vulnerabilities of those individuals it seeks to protect from harmful speech rather than on the contributions they make when properly recognized as equal members.

These concerns amount to pragmatic considerations for student groups to avoid calling for censorship of speech based on the point of view it represents. But this does not mean that their call for attention to the harm caused by speech and their efforts to create a more inclusive community with greater sensitivity to the impact of speech are altogether misguided or that they should be dismissed.

When some members of the campus community are effectively barred from speaking, when they avoid speaking their minds for fear of humiliation or ridicule, or when they do not feel that they belong or that they are appreciated, free speech is limited just as much as it can be limited by censorship. Defenders of free speech should be worried about both types of limits. They both make the debate poorer and hamper the democratic culture of campus, which is the framework that necessitates and justifies the commitment to free speech. Free speech arguments should not be wielded against demands for inclusion, and neither should claims of harm be lobbed at free speech. The common ground between the two sides is in fact much broader and more stable than either side assumes.

The claims that students make about harm, their demands for safety, and the counterclaims made in defense of free speech often fail to distinguish between *dignitary safety* and *intellectual safety*. Dignitary safety is the sense of being an equal member of the community and of being invited to contribute to a discussion as a valued participant. Dignitary safety and the avoidance of dignitary harms are necessary for the creation and maintenance of a democratic campus community. On the other hand, intellectual safety—the refusal to listen to challenges to one's views or to consider opposing viewpoints—is harmful to the open-minded inquiry that defines any university worth the name.

Challenging intellectual safety, or the attachment to one's unquestioned beliefs, must be done while maintaining conditions in which every student's dignity can be affirmed. This vision of education has long informed the kind of intellectual exploration that characterizes higher learning. In light of this long liberal tradition, the best education questions taken-for-granted habits of mind. It awakens, enlightens, and forces us to reconsider our assumptions and the foundations of our worldview. Thus the rejection of intellectual safety on college campuses is merely rephrasing the traditional protection of openness and honesty, sometimes at the price of rattling safe, accepted assumptions.

But the commitment to taking intellectual risks has nothing to do with some of the risks and harms that students attempt to prevent when they protest what they understand to be harmful forms of expression. It is both a cliché and an accurate claim that true ideas need testing by false ones lest they become mere prejudices and thoughtless slogans. A commitment to free speech is thus a crucial tool in the search for truth. However, the testing of true ideas must not in itself be done in a way that limits the freedom of speech and participation by those who can be harmed by these intellectual tests.

Ensuring that members of all groups are not only eligible for admission to college but are also able to take full advantage of the curriculum requires that colleges provide an environment safe from physical harm and that they do not dismiss the reality of dignitary harms. This tells us nothing about intellectual comfort, which will continue to be challenged. It also does not mean condoning the use of the blunt tools of censorship, "no platforming" rules, and bias reporting systems. Safety and the commitment to address harms ensure real—not merely formal—equal access.

It should be made clear that terms like "threat" and "harm" and calls for "safety" are not used as mere metaphors but rather reflect the experiences of students from many groups on many campuses who have honest and often well-grounded concerns about their physical well-being, as well as about the extent to which the campus community accepts them as equal members. The actual risks that some members of campus face are becoming more visible as a result of the increased diversity on campus, legal protections such as Title IX, and the willingness of students to listen to each other. Preventing those risks from looming over members of the campus community can be a shared goal of all who care about the democratic campus, whether they prioritize freedom or equality, as the inclusion of all members in an open debate is one of those instances where liberty and equality are both served. The newly widespread sensitivity to harm does not often stem from a rejection of the principles of freedom; rather, it arises from an increased commitment to equality. And indeed some members of stereotyped groups experience an onslaught of threats on campus—intellectual, physical, social, and sexual harms—as they try to make their way into the academic context from which their ancestors or predecessors were barred. Some of these threats to safety are illegal and should be dealt with as such. Others do not amount to illegality, but that does not mean that they should be dismissed. Establishing a campus culture committed to inclusive freedom requires attention to the various types of threats to students' belonging and substantive capacity to participate, and it therefore requires different levels of response from enforcing laws to developing a true and ongoing commitment to a diverse campus environment. It is important not to impinge on individuals' liberty while pursuing these goals. For instance, mandatory sensitivity training for all faculty members goes too far (and is also often ineffective). Building a campus culture that expresses commitment to equality is an ongoing task that will not be resolved by quick fixes. It requires a continual balancing act between competing values. Looking at those values where possible is a good start.

The events in Missouri are a case in point. Beginning in 2014, in line with the protests following the killing of Michael Brown in Ferguson, students at the University of Missouri formed a group called Concerned Student 1950, which began to coordinate protests and events highlighting the university's lack of response to incidents of racism on campus. (The date in the group's name derives from the year the first black student was admitted to the school.)

Some of the incidents to which the group drew attention included a swastika being drawn on a dorm wall, the student body president being called the n-word by several individuals in a passing pickup truck, and members of the Legion of Black Collegians having their rehearsal interrupted by a drunken white man also calling them the n-word. The group, which included students from various racial groups, was voicing a concern that minority students on campus experienced an ongoing series of attacks on their safety and on their sense of belonging and were constantly under threat of rejection, humiliation, and violence. Their goal was to change the campus atmosphere so that it would be more inclusive and welcoming and to create a greater sense of safety for all, and especially African American students.

Concerned Student 1950 reported that they had repeatedly reached out to President Tim Wolfe, asking for a response to incidents of this kind, and had been ignored. In protest, the group blocked the president's car at the homecoming parade and was removed by police. Following this incident, the group released a list of demands, chief of which was President Wolfe's resignation: "The students also demanded increasing black faculty and staff; mandatory racial awareness and inclusion curriculum for all staff, faculty, and students; and additional funding and resources for mental health professionals, particularly those of color, to boost campus programming and outreach to students."[14] Wolfe met with the group in response, but the meeting did not satisfy student protestors. A statement from the group described the character of the meeting: "Wolfe verbally acknowledged that he cared for black students at the University of Missouri, however he also reported he was 'not completely' aware of systemic racism, sexism, and patriarchy on campus."[15]

In a further attempt to get a clearer and more active response, on November 2, a twenty-five-year-old graduate student, Jonathan Butler, announced a hunger strike that he said he would not break unless Wolfe resigned. Wolfe released a statement on November 6 apologizing for how student protests at homecoming were handled and expressing concern for Butler's health. He added, "Racism does exist at our university, and it is unacceptable. It is a long-standing, systemic problem which daily affects our family of students, faculty, and staff."[16]

The following day, black members of the university football team announced that they would boycott their games in solidarity with Butler and Concerned Student until Wolfe resigned. This move would have cost the university one million dollars if it canceled the game against Brigham Young University.

As the events on campus gained more public attention, several politicians and lawmakers on both sides of the aisle spoke in support of the students. Back on campus, several members of the faculty also announced that they would be organizing a walkout.

In response, Wolfe announced his resignation, stating, "My motivation in making this decision comes from love. I love MU, Columbia, where I grew up, the state of Missouri. This is not the way change should come about." He added, though still taking some of the blame, "I take full responsibility for this frustration. I take full responsibility for this inaction."[17]

The demand for dignitary safety on campus in places like the University of Missouri—and on many other campuses—resulted from rising awareness of threats and harm. For members of some minority groups, which together make up the majority on campus and in society, the demand for recognition as intellectual equals in the classroom and as full members of the campus community is part of an effort to establish an overall sense of safety in a social context that is often unsafe. The affirmation of dignitary safety as a threshold condition for access should thus be understood not only as part of the psychological effort to reduce stereotype threats or the overall liberal effort to allow all members the necessary conditions to participate in shared intellectual pursuits; it should also be understood as part of the struggle against the marginalization of and assault against members of various groups in society. In this light, the demand for recognition should be seen as a way of ensuring the safety that is necessary for extending the reality of dignity to all members of the community and thus ensuring an open-minded exchange of ideas in all areas of the public sphere—including on campus—and an open and inclusive search for truth and knowledge.

Again it is Mill who reminds us that, by silencing a view, we harm the dignity of the speaker and that of her potential listeners. That is a strong reason to oppose censorship. But censorship is not the only way to silence; harsh treatment silences too. A sense of being rejected and ridiculed and fear for one's safety or standing can effectively push some students to avoid participating and speaking. Those committed to extending free speech to all on campus and to ensuring the democratic practice of open debate in search of the truth should do all they can to enable speech and to make sure that everyone in their community is able to contribute. However, the responsibility for creating a democratic campus culture should not be interpreted as a demand for any and all claims of harm to be unequivocally accepted. The notion of harm recognized through the inclusive freedom approach is broad and has subjective elements, but it should not lead to a culture of victimhood in which those who claim to be harmed always have the upper hand in policy debates. Instead, the broad notion of harm calls for an expanded set of tools to respond to harms experienced by students.

Dignitary safety in this context should be understood as an aspect of access. Limiting the access of members of a group merely because of gender, race, or other identity traits constitutes an unjustified harm to them and also impoverishes the academic environment for all. The hurdles and barriers that are unequally distributed across different groups in society must be recognized if we are to properly interpret the demand for dignitary safety. For many, the road to campus was long and fraught with difficulties that others never faced. For them to be forced to justify their presence, their eligibility, and their capacity to contribute is an insult added to injury.

It is easy to agree that the First Amendment provides historic, legal, and political contexts that should be respected and protected on campus. We should also be able to reach broad agreement on two additional principles that need to be reflected in debates on campus speech today and implemented appropriately to different campus communities. First, a commitment to open-minded inquiry and expression is at the heart of the college as an institution of learning, research, and service to the public. And second, this inquiry is most vibrant, most broad, and ultimately most successful when all are able to participate in it not only formally but also substantially.

Can Civility Ensure Participation?

When events on campus erupt into the public sphere in bursts of anger, blame, and mistrust, calls for civility are never far behind. Yet my own argument that free speech and inclusion should both be feasible goals rather than opposing visions should not be mistaken as a call for civility. Campus communities should not aspire to institute civility rules or aspire for a civil discussion on tough issues, especially not in the broader campus community. (Classroom interactions will be discussed in the next chapter.)

Civility requires both too little and too much: it requires too little in that it is based on norms of respectability and reasonableness rather than on substance (which could make it acceptable, for instance, to express racist views as long as it is done in a civil manner); it requires too much in that it further marginalizes those whose anger, frustration, and other emotions are deemed uncivil and thus unacceptable.

In September 2014, Nicholas Dirks, chancellor of the University of California, Berkeley, released a statement commemorating the fiftieth anniversary of the Free Speech Movement, in which his campus played a proud role. Somewhat surprisingly, he called for civility in the celebrations and in the exchange of ideas and views on campus: "We can only exercise our right to free speech insofar as we feel safe and respected in doing so, and this in turn requires that people treat each other with civility. Simply put, courteousness and respect in words and deeds are basic preconditions to any meaningful exchange of ideas. In this sense, free speech and civility are two sides of a single coin—the coin of open, democratic society."

Shortly afterward, Eric Barron, the president of Penn State, whose institution was embroiled in the child sexual abuse scandal involving the school's football team, released a video message to his own community deploring the erosion of civility in university discourse: "Respect is a core value at Penn State . . . we ask you to consciously choose civility and to support those whose words and actions serve to promote respectful disagreement and thereby strengthen our community."[18]

Civility represents an effort to reconcile the tensions between protecting liberty on the one hand and maintaining an inclusive community on the other; in relation to the terms used here, it is a suggested middle ground between free speech and dignitary safety. But civility falls short of this goal, because it leans too strongly to the side of order, reasonableness, and avoidance of challenge. To protect inclusive free speech, much more room should be made for messy, inappropriate, challenging, and sometimes uncivil expression.

The demands of civility parallel the current discussion on political correctness. Opponents of "PC culture" claim that overly sensitive millennials are leading a ridiculous effort to cleanse language and corresponding social norms and culture of any reference to differences among social groups. In other words, they view PC as a way to protect the indifference and laziness of thought that characterize intellectual safety—the refusal to take intellectual risks or consider different opinions, viewpoints, and positions. Proponents see PC culture, or some restrictions on offensive speech, as a way to create a space where all are appreciated and welcome and enjoy an environment in which their contributions and questions are appreciated rather than ridiculed. They see (certain forms of) political correctness as a way to ensure dignitary safety for all.

Civility thus does not resolve many issues of contentious speech, nor does it allow everyone to air their views, concerns, and grievances. Even parliaments are often not civil, so why would campuses be? The attempt to institute civil practices of dialogue and debate is meant to maintain the decorum of proper conversation. However, the demand that members of the campus community behave in a civil way and express their views according to civil norms of conversation can in fact dampen free speech. Civility, which can be seen as a foundational dimension

71

of a democratic open marketplace of ideas, can be used and has been used to limit speech based on viewpoint; it also can too easily be translated into a set of requirements for proper expression that chills the free (and sometimes emotional or rowdy) exchange of ideas that characterizes an open campus environment.

To reconcile the tensions that inevitably arise in a diverse and open environment, campuses should rely on responses rooted in democratic principles rather than in calls for proper and civil exchange. It is too easy for Catholic universities to restrict the activities of pro-choice student groups as uncivil and improper or for Fordham University to refuse students' request to start a chapter of Students for Justice in Palestine on similar grounds.

In his denial, the Fordham University's dean of students gave the following explanation:

> While students are encouraged to promote diverse political points of view, and we encourage conversation and debate on all topics, I cannot support an organization whose sole purpose is advocating political goals of a specific group, and against a specific country, when these goals clearly conflict with and run contrary to the mission and values of the University.
>
> There is perhaps no more complex topic than the Israeli-Palestinian conflict, and it is a topic that often leads to polarization rather than dialogue. The purpose of the organization as stated in the proposed club constitution points toward that polarization. Specifically, the call for Boycott, Divestment and Sanctions of Israel presents a barrier to open dialogue and mutual learning and understanding.[19]

The response statement from Fordham University's faculty represents a contrary and productive approach: "Those of us signing this petition have a range of opinions on issues related to Israel and Palestine, and on the best approach to addressing those issues. Some of us firmly oppose the Boycott, Divestment, and Sanctions movement (BDS); some of us strongly support it; some of us hold other views. But we all agree that this decision violates basic principles . . . Students' freedom of speech and freedom of association, including the freedom to advocate for a cause, are central to academic freedom. And academic freedom is a value we treasure as faculty members."[20]

The politics of civility and respectability tends, in particular, to implicate marginalized groups and charge them with playing a role in their own marginalization, based on their presumed willful failure to adhere by norms of civility.[21] This charge echoes the vicious cycle described in the previous chapter as "epistemic injustice," or the refusal to recognize the validity of certain standpoints because of the identities of those who advocate them. Clearly, some basic democratic laws and norms that are often included within the notion of civility, such as avoiding violence, need to be respected for a productive exchange of ideas to take place. But civility tends to demand more, and thus it should be carefully considered, especially in the context of exchanging ideas in public spaces on campus (as differentiated from the classroom). If students on the campus main walkway or plaza dance to draw attention to their play, dress in unusual ways to make a statement, or express their anger over policies or political events by staging sit-ins and die-ins, all these can too easily be deemed "uncivil" and therefore curbed. Open expression should be protected under broader terms than proper decorum, and demands for civility often play a negative role in the effort to protect speech on campus.

As noted, inclusive freedom calls on campus communities to agree on two key principles that underlie the main mission of colleges and universities today. First, a commitment to teaching and research can only be fulfilled in the context of an open-minded and intellectually honest environment. If truth and knowledge are to be pursued, speech and other modes of expression must be protected to the broadest extent possible. Second, all members of the campus community must know that they are invited to participate in this pursuit. Ensuring that all can develop and express their views in an open atmosphere requires adhering to key democratic principles, nondiscrimination being the main one among them. Therefore, a campus committed to democracy in all its mess and glory—a commitment to democracy that encompasses individual rights and collective identities, that recognizes and grapples with power differentials and the need for equity—must be aware of the importance of free speech, not in a neutral way but with attention to the context and effect of words. Protecting expression is a means of protecting ideas; the protection of ideas, in turn, demands that we understand the social, historical, and political contexts in which they are uttered. It calls on all members, especially those with greater power (e.g., campus administrators, faculty, larger student groups) to preserve the equality of all members of the campus community as they develop and express their views and as they clash with opposing views. Recognition of the equal membership of all participants in the campus community requires—similar to the principle of free inquiry—an open and inclusive debate about matters that different constituents on campus may want to raise and discuss.

How does this argument translate to an institutional setting? The threshold conditions for intellectual engagement include various forms of access. Formal access is the basic condition an institution needs to satisfy in order to create an environment where open exchange is encouraged. In the past, denial of access was common among higher education institutions for members of many groups, such as women and various minorities. Inviting members of all groups to join the institution is a first step.

Beyond formal permission to apply, a prospective student needs to have the required credentials too—a high school diploma, appropriate SAT scores, and the like. Members of many groups see their access as limited by structural hurdles to achieving these requirements. The debate on affirmative action and class- or race-conscious admissions policies is tied to efforts to overcome these structural barriers, and it parallels the current debate in its search for conditions that allow equality for all.

Finally, once a student arrives on campus, having been permitted to apply as a member of her group (e.g., women, people of color, noncitizens) and found to be eligible in terms of her credentials, one last hurdle (or set of hurdles) remains. The threshold for full participation for students involves the less tangible but no less real requirement of fitting in with the norms and expectations on campus and in the classrooms. The focus should not be on civility as a main norm but rather on the conditions for dignitary safety, whose absence limits the substantive access of some members of the community. Even within a civil classroom, without dignitary safety, students fear humiliation, ridicule, and rejection and are therefore partially or wholly barred from taking full advantage of their learning opportunities.

Deciding when, if ever, the harm done or risked is significant enough to justify putting a limitation on the free exchange of ideas can be difficult, especially when the harmed party is a young person whose identity and skills are evolving and whose well-being is entrusted to the university along with the role of expanding his mind. Again, some issues in this area are easier than others. Protecting a student's intellectual comfort by avoiding serious challenges to her views may create a sense of well-being and safety, but the price paid in development and in the opportunity to participate in the university's mission would be too high to pay. On the other hand, when the challenges presented to a student are based not on shaking her beliefs or views but rather on undermining her dignity and questioning whether she belongs in the institution altogether—especially as a member of an identity group—this can damage not only her sense of well-being but also the ability of others to hear her and evaluate her views. The guiding principles for drawing this line should be based on a democratic commitment to inclusive freedom rather than on principles of civility.

Consider the demand that the names of buildings be changed when they honor historical figures whose legacy includes the moral stain of support for slavery or an active participation in it. Such demands came up at Yale regarding John C. Calhoun[22] and at Princeton regarding

Woodrow Wilson.[23] These names and the historical meaning that is attached to them have long become invisible to many on campus. Raising the matter is a way to reengage with the arguments for and against giving this particular honor to an individual, to discuss his legacy, and to revisit his place in the history of the institution and the nation. While this can be an uncomfortable process, especially for those who support the existing name (and for those who no longer notice it), such discomfort should not be seen as a reason to avoid the conversation. As is often rightly noted, intellectual safety does not support a truthful and productive discussion.

With this in mind, the discussion on campus speech should start with a commitment to free speech that includes as one of its aspects a commitment to providing true equal access to all members of a college community. Speech should be recognized as an action that can promote or curtail the ability of all members of the community to participate in fulfilling the university's mission. Calls for civility in the exercise of free speech can too easily be used to suppress and exclude others by posing requirements of decorum and politeness and demands about content of speech, focusing on what can permissibly be discussed "in polite company." Instead, inclusive freedom should be satisfied with what Teresa Bejan calls "mere civility," or the minimal, even begrudging norms of respectful behavior needed to keep a conversation going.[24]

Speech on campus should thus be informed by bedrock democratic values, including a commitment to the truth, open-mindedness, mutual respect, and nondiscrimination. That may sound like a long list, but it is in fact no more than the very basic, minimal norms required to sustain an ongoing dialogue without indignity or censorship. Those values and norms should be framed by the expanding goals of higher education institutions: preparation for public and civic leadership roles, the development of intellectual honesty and curiosity, and readiness for a variety of jobs both in skills and in mindset. By ensuring that all members of the campus community are not silenced or excluded, the campus can expand the boundaries of free speech and therefore enhance its ability to pursue and disseminate knowledge. Respect does not equal limited speech; it provides an opportunity to listen and to learn, to push the boundaries of knowledge, to ask questions that were not asked before or have not been considered for a while, and to look for answers in new places. All these elements are at the core of the university's mission, and the increasing diversity of students and faculty, as well as the increased attention to matters raised by diverse groups on campus should be welcomed by faculty and administration as opportunities to express and strengthen the university's commitment to open-mindedness, public-mindedness, cutting-edge research, and excellent teaching.

The Virtual Quad: Campus Free Speech Online

Online communication presents a growing set of challenges to those engaged in the effort to protect and respond to free speech on campus. Anonymity, wide dissemination, and other characteristics of online speech demand a more careful response beyond the mere application of free speech principles to online modes of communications.[25]

Some recent challenging cases, such as provocative statements made by faculty on Twitter, offensive remarks about a student in an anonymous group chat, and the distribution of embarrassing pictures without permission, point to the need to develop and encourage norms of digital communication and horizontal accountability (as distinct from top-down management) in campus communities as they interact and represent themselves in the virtual public sphere.

Communication on social media and through various online platforms creates unique challenges to campus communities that strive to protect an open exchange of ideas in an inclusive and open-minded environment. Some of the unique characteristics of online platforms make it hard for both individuals and institutions to ensure that all can express their views. Specifically, some platforms permit anonymity and thus preclude vertical or centralized accountability for speech, a characteristic that sets them apart from other modes of communication. Online communication can more readily become widespread or viral and can leave a more permanent mark in comparison to in-person speech. Some platforms create echo chambers that make it harder for individuals to consider opposing views, and the lack of accountability can encourage some people to express unsavory views. Extreme views draw more and stronger responses, encouraging some to engage in stronger forms of expression. From an administrative standpoint, it also matters that most platforms are not owned or operated by the university, and therefore online speech (outside of sponsored platforms like campus mail) is for the most part out of reach to campus administrators.

In recent years, many challenging campus speech cases have involved online modes of communication, especially social media. When students and professors express views on social media, they sometimes assume that they are speaking just to their friends (or "friends," "followers," or other contacts on the platform they are using), and sometimes they let down their guard or try to speak more provocatively. In the summer of 2014, Steven Salaita, an associate professor of English, was preparing to move to the University of Illinois Urbana-Champaign (UIUC) to start a new job there. As war was raging that summer in Gaza between Israeli and Palestinian troops, Salaita took to Twitter to harshly condemn Israel for its responsibility for the many civilian casualties on the Palestinian side. In response, UIUC's board refused to approve his contract.[26]

The legal dispute is beyond the current discussion (suffice it to say that UIUC settled the matter by offering Salaita significant compensation), but it is worth mentioning this case because it puts into sharp relief the unique issues posed by social media and other online forms of expression. Is a view expressed on social media akin to a conversation among friends—in which case, it can hardly ever be regulated? Is it more akin to a published article or an editorial on traditional media and thus subject to clearer substantive, methodological, and stylistic expectations? And if students are exposed to it, should it be seen as equivalent in some way to classroom speech? These questions were presented in all their force in the Salaita case, again in the case of an Oberlin professor who posted anti-Semitic views on Facebook,[27] and in various less widely publicized cases.

The matter is not much easier when student speech is involved: male athletes who share vile comments about female peers in closed groups or on message boards, cheerleaders who post racist pictures on Snapchat, and frat members who post pictures in blackface have all been subjected to intense attention and sometimes also punishment.[28] The tension between protecting free speech and maintaining an inclusive and hospitable environment is further complicated by, on the one hand, the university's goal of avoiding being perceived as endorsing or permitting distasteful or hateful speech and, on the other, the near impossibility—both practically and as a matter of democratic values—of monitoring all online speech by members of the campus community, which makes the instances of hateful speech caught and punished seem arbitrary.

Some characteristics of online expression point in the direction of requiring clear guidelines and maybe regulation; whether written, photographic, audio, or videotaped, the speech is more permanent than oral speech tends to be and, in this sense, is more akin to traditional publication and thus subject to similar expectations of veracity and professionalism. Online speech is also often more broadly accessible, either because it is posted in shareable formats or because it can be shared with others even if the speaker did not intend for it to reach a wider audience. On the other hand, online expression is quite similar to plain or conversational speech in that it is often casual or informal, requires little preparation or planning, and can be perceived as occurring "among friends." Due to the specific characteristics of various platforms—such as allowing anonymity (or false identities), a sense of control over past content (including editing or deleting previous expressions), and the ability to respond to and solicit responses from a wide range of potential listeners—it is clear that online speech is not fully comparable to other forms and contexts of speech. It therefore cannot simply be suggested that speech online is akin to any other speech when it comes to regulating, protecting, or responding to it.

I cannot hope to develop here a full account of how to respond to online speech by campus members, simply because this is not in itself a form of campus speech, and therefore colleges and universities should recognize that online speech for the most part is beyond their purview. In some cases, campus administrators are pulled into a debate over online statements made by members of their communities, as the examples above show. Some events like these can draw significant responses from different audiences, including alumni, students and their parents, and the media. The fact that extreme or hateful speech and sometimes expressions of political ideologies in striking forms can generate strong reactions and demands for action should not drive campus administrators to ban or censor speech. Posts on social media platforms like Facebook are not campus speech, as Facebook is an independent company, even as interactions or expressions on social media can impact campus relations; social media platforms do not use campus servers and cannot reasonably be seen as a service that belongs to the college. For the most part, online speech should be seen as separate from campus speech.

In some cases, online speech could merit reprimand— for example, when an athletic director sees the communication among team members as part of the team's shared work and as standing in opposition to the values they hope to promote. The response can mostly be reactive because the platforms and modes of possible expression are evolving rapidly and there is no point in trying to anticipate and regulate them ahead of time; doing so would also be contradictory to the democratic message that the campus should uphold. Therefore, while online speech cannot fully be subsumed under the guidelines that organize free speech on campus, it can still be seen as part of what the campus community aims to achieve.[29] In those limited instances when a campus reasonably decides to take steps in response to unwanted forms of online expression, those actions should be based on the same values that inform inclusive freedom—namely, a protection of legally allowed speech and a strong commitment to protecting democratic values while creating an inclusive community.

Putting Civility in Its Place

Free Speech in the Classroom

Students come to college primarily to learn; while colleges are often in the headlines these days when speech and political issues arise, in fact political expression and civic development are not the main purposes of college. Most of the speech cases discussed so far, and those that animate public debate, occur outside of class, but it is inside the four walls of the classroom that the most meaningful and productive opportunities for discussion, the development of knowledge, and the free exchange of ideas take place. In what ways is speech protected in the classroom today, and how does the inclusive freedom framework affect teaching and learning on campus? Academic freedom protects much of what happens within the classroom, and it is more central and more significant to the functioning of the university than the general guidelines, where those are available, organizing free speech. This chapter considers the need for distinctions between responding to speech inside and outside the classroom, differences in the notion of safety in these two distinct contexts, and a way to preserve access and dignity in class. I consider how cases involving tensions about speech that arise during class can be addressed within an inclusive freedom framework. I examine the importance of not only allowing but encouraging and managing student speech in class, and I comment on the incentives for and the dangers of instituting a civility regime that avoids conflict by discouraging impassioned speech. I also offer alternative civil yet engaged classroom practices.

Applying the framework of inclusive freedom inside the classroom requires another look at the distinction between intellectual safety and harm on the one hand and dignitary safety and harm on the other. In the classroom, intellectual safety should be rejected to allow openminded research and teaching to take place, and intellectual harm, such as the harm caused by inaccurate and misleading speech, should be regulated. At the same time, dignitary safety should be protected as a way to ensure full access to campus by all members. Such protection includes attention to forms of speech and responses to them while refraining from strictly regulating or curtailing speech. In what follows, I consider what these principles would mean to the professors' (or instructors') speech and expression, and then to the students' expression, in class.

The Professor Speaks: Academic Freedom and Freedom of Expression

Academic freedom gives professors broad discretion over expressions and interactions in the classroom. Free speech guidelines and First Amendment protections permit students to speak their minds too, but they offer very limited guidance as to how classrooms should operate. While professors should obviously work within free speech parameters in the classroom, there are two additional principles that should guide their work: the first intellectual and the second civic. First, as part of their commitment to teaching—developing and disseminating knowledge—instructors are bound by intellectual honesty in ways that can in fact limit their expression. For example, they must not lie in class, even as free speech permits them to lie; they must focus on the relevant and important subject matter, even as free speech allows them to read their favorite poems rather than teach. In other words, academic freedom is more demanding and more limiting than free speech rules, and it is academic freedom, rather than the more general contours of free speech, that should guide classroom (and lab and clinic) work. Second, college teaching should contribute to the development of civic skills and values. These civic goals can be more or less central in different classrooms—an introductory lecture hall in biology would be different from a small seminar in politics or a constitutional law class—but in all these, instructors are never solely transmitters of knowledge. A good college education would include at least some—and ideally many—instructors who see themselves not only as teaching in their field but also as educators who prepare their students for their broader roles in society. In this regard, instructors should devote some thought to the ways in which dissent, harm, and other forms of expression can present themselves in the classroom and how they might productively respond to free speech challenges.

The goal of work in the classroom is learning—namely, the development, exchange, and transmission of knowledge. To achieve this goal, the ground rules in class have to include a commitment to intellectual honesty, which requires adherence to discipline-appropriate, scientific- and evidence-based practices. When learning about climate, there is no room for questioning scientific evidence, even if one's ideological position runs counter to the information laid out in class. Similarly, there is no need to accommodate religious or ideological objections to accepted knowledge. But in practice, that does not mean that objections should be silenced; in many cases, shutting down speech is neither justified nor an effective way of countering intellectual dishonesty or inaccurate perceptions. Oftentimes the instructor can think ahead about what opposing arguments might be raised and plan effective ways to engage with them, which is not only more respectful but also more productive as a teaching method.

This does not mean that instructors should, or do, promote ideological views in class. Politicians are sometimes concerned that colleges are promoting a liberal ideology, a perception enhanced by surveys, such as one indicating that 32 percent of first-year students considered themselves liberal or far left, compared with 60 percent of faculty members.[1] While this concern may be understandable, it must not result in political interventions into academic work. In 2016, the Wisconsin state legislature demanded information about syllabi used in Wisconsin's public university system. The sentiment leading to this demand was summarized in statements such as, "Ideological conformity has been institutionalized on the nation's campuses. Students are encouraged to look upon American society from a perspective of righteous indignation."[2] The legislators zeroed in on a course about "whiteness" as a reason to defund or otherwise punish public universities in the state. They seemed to presume that the course represented an attack on white people and an attempt to elevate ethnic and racial minorities over whites and that it was a waste or misuse of public dollars to fund the instruction of such a course. Without looking at the merits of the course itself, which are immaterial to the discussion, it should be clear that the legislature should not have had the power to censor or otherwise affect the content of teaching. Similar attacks on free speech in college—including in the classroom—in the name of moral and political views are becoming more common: various colleges are also instituting "bias reporting systems," whereby committees are set up to invite and investigate students' reports on their professors' speech in the classroom. Students may worry about discriminatory or ideological expressions the professors make in class, but such reporting systems are bound to chill speech and harmfully limit teaching and learning, especially among untenured (or non-tenure-track) professors whose jobs are not secure.

The response to such attacks on academic freedom should be an unwavering commitment to protecting the broadest possible range of teaching and research. When professors are protected and free to plan their classes, expose students to knowledge, and invite them to contribute to the process, they can present unpopular views and question current perspectives. This process has to be open if it is to advance knowledge rather than simply repeat accepted orthodoxies without question. It has to be done while preserving open access to the classroom by inviting all students, independent of their identities, current views, or beliefs, to participate in the process. Protecting free speech requires that faculty consider a broad range of relevant views and that they are protected when making decisions about classroom materials. Students on more liberal campuses who feel marginalized because of their conservative or other right-leaning political ideologies should sense that their views are respected and valued whether or not they are reflected in a particular syllabus. Minority students on mostly white campuses should feel the same.

Polarization on campus and concerns about losing control over the lesson plan or class discussion can lead professors to avoid controversy as much as possible. This is even more likely when the professor in question is not a tenured member of the faculty. Tenured (and tenure-track) faculty are becoming a smaller share of the faculty overall, and many of the instructors that students see in class have limited job security and academic protections. The urge to avoid controversy as a way of protecting one's job, of adhering to the lesson plan, or simply of avoiding the possible tensions that might arise when one wades into touchy, painful, or charged topics is understandable. It also must be overcome.

In many fields, teaching difficult topics is unavoidable. Some law professors have become careful about teaching rape laws,[3] for example, but this is clearly not a viable solution when one is charged with training lawyers. Controversial topics come up when teaching history, engineering, business, or philosophy. Treading around them is intellectually dishonest; (some) lawyers need to know about rape laws, history students should be able to address colonialism or nationalism, and students in professional schools need to understand ethical controversies in their fields.

But intellectual honesty is only one reason to make charged topics a part of the lesson plan. One other reason is that a college does more than train professionals in specific fields, and its role goes beyond that of a vocational program. Higher education institutions are always responsible as well for training citizens who are almost inevitably going to be part of society by contributing to its development as leaders, professional experts, and civic participants. Shying away from controversy in the college classroom (and in college more generally) by stemming speech and averting debate teaches students that there is no proper way to disagree, no room for considering other opinions, and no way to bridge the gap between opposing views. Delving into controversial issues (including those that are politically charged), scientific disagreements, and other difficult topics is key to the education of both researchers and citizens.

This kind of engagement by no means requires a rejection of sound pedagogical practices—including, in some cases, indications in class or on the syllabus that painful and difficult topics are ahead. "Trigger warnings" themselves have become a controversial topic in recent years, despite having had a long-standing quiet presence in many courses for years. The controversial August 2016 letter by the dean of students to freshmen at the University of Chicago specifically addressed trigger warnings, stating, "Our commitment to academic freedom means that we do not support so-called 'trigger warnings.'"[4]

The response penned by faculty members raised an important objection: "Those of us who have signed this letter have a variety of opinions about requests for trigger warnings and safe spaces. We may also disagree as to whether free speech is ever legitimately interrupted by concrete pressures of the political. That is as it should be. But let there be no mistake: such requests often touch on substantive, ongoing issues of bias, intolerance, and trauma that affect our intellectual exchanges. To start a conversation by declaring that such requests are not worth making is an affront to the basic principles of liberal education and participatory democracy."[5]

The position expressed by the faculty members is sound, and as is clear from their letter, it stems from experience in the classroom rather than an effort to respond to political demands or to carve a niche of intellectual honesty within an imagined sea of intolerance and prudery. An instructor will be smart to let her students know what is coming ahead in a course so that they can decide how to prepare and even whether participating is in their best interest. Intellectual candor does not demand springing surprises on students to see how they respond or how resilient they are. Preparing for class requires reading the material, thinking ahead, and planning. Trigger warnings—or whatever else one might call the courteous forewarning by a professor ("tough topic ahead!")—should be seen as a matter of good pedagogy and academic practice rather than a surrender to weakness and laziness of thought. In most cases, there is no need or strong justification to permit students to avoid a class because of its "triggering"—painful, traumatic, harmful—content, but sometimes that allowance is acceptable. It's a small price for a criminal law class to pay if a student who suffered trauma avoids class discussion on rape laws. She would still need to pass the same requirements and do the same (or equivalent) work as decided in consultation with her professor. Deriding her for her difficulty does nothing to improve the discussion or strengthen her knowledge and educational experience. On the other hand, expanding the demand for trigger warnings to include exemptions from classes or assignments for trivial reasons undermines the overall justified cause of this pedagogic mechanism.

Political and civic skills and dispositions develop best in structured contexts like school and college classrooms, in which controversial topics are discussed in an engaged and respectful manner and in which people feel empowered to express their views and consider different positions.[6] In many cases, this is also a practical way to increase engagement and therefore improve learning. Introducing controversial topics in a planned and thoughtful way supports the development of informed, critical, and engaged citizens and is an integral part of the ethics of pedagogy in higher education contexts.[7] Clearly, the main location where such efforts should take place is the K–12 classroom, where almost all future citizens can benefit from it (rather than only those who make it to college). Still, college classrooms can provide a significant context for similar development. To the extent that they provide spaces for interaction with peers and institutional authorities and contexts for increasing knowledge and expertise, they help develop some civic skills and dispositions, even if that is not their main goal. Therefore, it is best to be conscious about the kinds of opportunities afforded in class for students to become engaged and especially to develop and express their views and listen to those of others.

In the concluding chapter, I suggest some practical ways to plan and organize an inclusive classroom environment that is committed to the protection of free speech. For now I would just note broadly that to facilitate such a context, it is best not to avoid controversy—neither when the professor brings it up nor when students raise controversial issues. It is likewise important not to let the controversy get out of control, taking over the lesson plan or damaging the relationships among students or between students and their instructor. Containing the process of discussing controversial issues makes it possible to have an open and free exchange while avoiding both dignitary and intellectual harms.

It is important to note that these considerations are not limited to classrooms where texts are being interpreted or historical significance and meaning of events are being debated. While it is easy to see how humanities and social sciences classrooms can readily implement suggestions related to critical thinking and discussion in class, opportunities abound—and are urgently required—in the classrooms of other disciplines. Some of the most challenging free speech concerns that administrators encounter have to do with professors who teach climate science and are concerned about some students' expression of doubt and with students in the medical professions who suggest that some of their professors stigmatize ethnic groups as culpable for health challenges. Early during the AIDS epidemic in the United States, when the scope of the tragedy was not widely known and it was commonly termed Gay-Related Immune Deficiency (GRID), research was hampered by competing ideological standpoints that prevented the development of accurate knowledge of the deadly disease. Conservatives—including President Ronald Reagan—seemed to assume that this was an illness limited to the gay community and borne of promiscuity or other moral failings and thus did not deserve the public's attention, whereas some advocates, including gay physicians, rejected the possibility that this new mysterious illness could be tied to a new virus.[8]

There were various reasons for this rejection, but some were related to the concern that if such a virus were to be discovered and related to homosexuality in some way, it would be seen by adversaries of the gay community as justification for physical and public attacks or for quarantine of suspected carriers (as in fact happened during the early years of the epidemic). Some gay liberation advocates refused to consider the possibility that promiscuity or unprotected sex with multiple partners could be causing or exacerbating the epidemic. Only the open-minded and professional commitment of many researchers, citizens, gay advocates, and HIV/AIDS patients allowed for the epidemic to begin to be understood and treated. It is disheartening to realize that the good intentions of some advocates who worked to reject the association between homosexuality and social and physical ills may have been one of the hurdles on the way to understanding the epidemic in its early stages (though it by no means was a main reason for the prolonged delay in developing treatment). Hence an open and inclusive inquiry that takes into account the perspectives of those affected along with other views and seeks the truth beyond prejudice and orthodoxies of thought can push forward knowledge in a broad range of fields from the humanities classroom to the lab.

The Students Speak

Given that discussion is a key tool for engaging students, allowing them to express and extend their involvement in subject matter while helping them develop their civic capacities, it is helpful to think ahead about what these discussions should look like.

Many commentators point to civility as a key concept around which conversational ground rules can be set, mostly because civility seems to preclude intolerant expressions and therefore prevent the pitfalls of harm and hurt that are the immediate risks of a candid conversation unlimited by strict civility demands. As noted earlier, civility in itself is not a useful tool for protecting free speech, supporting an inclusive and free inquiry, or enabling the development of open-mindedness and engagement in class.

In class, civility justly forbids outright mocking, racist and misogynic declarations, and physical harm. However, it still permits "muted and surreptitious attitudes of disdain"[9] that serve as the basic currency of dignitary harms and as an effective and persistent mechanism of shutting members of marginalized groups out of the conversation. The widespread sense of members of newer groups—women, first-generation students, members of many minority groups—that they do not belong or that they are imposters is (at least in part) a result of messages expressed through these "acceptable" muted responses to their contributions or even to their presence.

Moreover, the civility expectation of the college classroom, if and when it is implemented, prioritizes what is traditionally seen as proper behavior and restricts expressions of emotions like anger, frustration, and disaffection. Seen from a historical perspective, civility seems to allow only "appropriate," noble forms of expression to count as civil, whereas those that are traditionally ascribed to women and to "lesser" cultures—excitement, anger, tears—continue to be rejected and censored. In this respect, it leaves limited tools in the hands of those who continue to suspect that they are still treated as less than full members. Civility constrains speech, which is one strike against it; another strike is that it replicates exclusive practices without providing students with the breadth of expression they could use in class. Neither does it clarify how the discussion should proceed when harm or hurt occurs.

Rejecting civility as the guiding principle does not mean that the classroom need not have ground rules related to both conversational practices and desirable content to ensure the opportunity for all to participate in a productive and focused discussion on the issues at hand, as deemed relevant (at least initially) by the professor. Inclusive freedom aims to limit the possibility that students will be restricted from expressing their views and questions in class, including preventing to the best extent possible their exclusion from participation due to harm related to speech they hear in class from the professor or their peers.

Clearly, lesson plans often call for focus on a particular topic. Should students be permitted to raise challenges to the content of class, based on their beliefs? Should a professor engage with a student in her class who is questioning the validity of scientific knowledge about climate change? There are two main reasons to consider doing so: the first based on intellectual commitments and the second based on dignitary ones.

First, unsubstantiated views are endorsed by many in broader society, and indeed some of them are relatively widespread. By dismissing them, we do little to counter their hold on some minds, and in that we neglect our obligation to disseminate accurate and reliable information. Not only does the student who brings up perspectives such as climate-change denial remain set in her views, but the professor also misses an opportunity to illustrate to other students how one might respond to questions like this, which they might face in the course of their professional and civic lives. Having a model or blueprint for how to respond is useful for other students as they develop their knowledge and skills, and therefore should be seen as an opportunity for learning rather than as a waste of valuable class time.

Moreover, shutting down a student who raises an objection to the content presented in class might constitute harm to the student's dignity, which is a concern as a matter of principle as well as in regard to its effects. The student might raise the concern innocently, or she might be politically motivated to try to get a rise out of the professor or her classmates. It is sometimes hard to judge in the moment what the motivation might be. Usually, it is advisable to assign the best motivations to students unless they have proven otherwise. It is better to assume students have innocuous or positive motivations than mistakenly to ascribe to them negative goals that they do not in fact espouse, like disruption or empty challenges. A response from a professor who presumes the student to be earnest is more likely to preserve the student's dignity and therefore her inclination to continue expressing herself in class. A student who raises a significant, if misguided, objection to a topic that is part of the lesson plan should most commonly be treated with respect and his position receive due consideration, at least briefly. It is clearly not always possible to take up class time to consider objections to the material. It might be too disruptive or too irrelevant, or the time might not suffice. The objection also may not have the intellectual merits to justify a disruption of the lesson plan. This still is not a reason to reject the speaker in ways that harm his dignity. Inasmuch as dignity is a necessary condition for the student to be able to access the curriculum and the learning in class, it is important to preserve his dignity even when his specific comment, dissent, or question is being put aside. Some cases are easier than others. Climate-change denial may be an easy case because it is clear enough to the professor and hopefully to most others in class where the truth can be found. The main challenge is how to clarify the correct position to a student who holds an incorrect one.

But what about political rather than evidence-based views? For some liberals and progressives—who are the majority among the faculty—issues such as marriage equality hold the same moral force as factual claims do, in that their validity cannot be denied and counterarguments should be patently rejected. Some on the left seem to suggest that political, religious, or moral objections to liberal positions regarding equality or social justice can and should be dismissed or even shut down so as to preserve both truth and access. For many on the left, voicing opposition to marriage equality is reprehensible. An opposition to allowing trans people to use the bathroom of their choice indicates a rejection of their equal rights and is thus a form of bigotry. But opposing views are common on the conservative right and beyond, making the tension between groups espousing these opposing views raw and sometimes explosive. These have to be accommodated in the classroom in contexts where they are relevant because the classroom offers a productive context for exploring them and considering opportunities for exchanging ideas. This can be done within ground rules that respect all members of the class, including those who are members of the discussed groups, as well as both those who support and those who oppose the specific accommodations. Shutting down speech to protect accepted views from political challenges is an affront to free speech as well as to the requirements of intellectual honesty, which demand that professors recognize political opposition when discussing controversial topics. The protection of marginalized groups from harm can and should be considered within the context of the discussion.

Objections to topics raised in class are not the only way students can create concerns about free speech in class. What about students who demean others? Or students who raise questions that not only challenge the facts the professor was presenting ("Stem cells are not in fact a useful tool for curing disease") but also challenge the dignity or fitness of their peers ("Poor people don't actually care about education; that's why they remain poor")? Elizabeth Anderson considers the case of a student who, unimpressed by an African American peer's question in class, states, "That's what you get with affirmative action."[10] She suggests that it is sometimes reasonable to silence students who breach classroom norms or democratic expectations by making racist or other hateful statements.[11] Their candor may come at too high a price. But silencing would be justified only after making an honest effort to understand the offending student's view or at the very least engaging with him so as not to leave his offensive comment unanswered. An instructor should not expect the offended student to resolve the matter, especially when—as in this case—the affront to his dignity is based on his identity.

It is never appropriate for a professor or a fellow student to call upon a specific student to represent an identity group to which he or she belongs or is presumed to belong. Being the one minority student in class is burden enough. Being asked to represent "the African American view" or "the Muslim perspective" on a certain matter constitutes both an intellectual harm (because there is not a view that would be shared across all members of an identity group) and a dignitary harm because, at that moment, the student is not viewed as a person but rather as a symbol, reduced to one aspect of his humanity for the others' purpose.

Similarly, it is inadvisable to make assumptions about what "we" in the room think. This is a common practice by both professors and students, and it often inadvertently excludes and shames. If during a class discussion in a selective college a student says, "We all come from privileged backgrounds," she is casually demanding that some in the class clarify that they grew up in poverty or else remain silent and "pass" as more privileged than they are. It is the instructor's responsibility to correct statements like these, which often are innocent or ignorant rather than malicious. When instructors or students assume that all in class share the same ideology, those who have different views are pressured to remain silent or to present a clear opposition, both uncomfortable options. Assuming a broader "we" in class can resolve this tension and thus improve the quality of discussion.

The goal of these suggestions and additional ones offered in the conclusion is not to regulate or limit speech. An open, wide-ranging, inclusive atmosphere is a necessary condition for learning. No student (or instructor) should feel that she needs to monitor her words, worry about retaliation, or fear an explosive exchange. Rather than using administrative or legal tools to monitor speech, it is better to use pedagogic tools for thinking, planning, and managing a productive discussion in class, one that is informed by intellectual honesty and courage as well as a commitment to creating an inclusive environment. An inclusive environment should be seen as conducive to intellectual honesty because when all are welcome to participate in the conversation, each student can better learn. If some are assumed to be unfit or are casually rejected from the debate, the debate itself becomes poorer.

Applying the framework of inclusive freedom to the college classroom does not mean developing a set of stringent and detailed PC guidelines about what should not be said. Inclusive freedom calls on professors to develop explicit classroom ground rules that focus on engagement and inclusion and directs the students to think critically about the subject matter and to listen to both their instructors and their classmates. Speech codes in class are unhelpful, but creating an inclusive environment by setting clear expectations is hardly a high price to pay for the open-minded and inclusive pursuit of knowledge.

Conclusion and
Practical Guidelines

The mission of colleges and universities has expanded in recent decades along with the makeup of the campus population. Along with this changed population and mission, the forms of communication taking place on campus have multiplied in the contexts of teaching and learning, conducting research, and expressing personal and political views. The campus accommodates more diverse groups and needs to account for a greater variety of views when holding a multitude of events from holiday celebrations to graduation. In this respect, free speech on campus is not just another instance of free speech in the public sphere of a democratic nation. It is a special case in a special context, and understanding the complexities can help ease some of the recent tensions around allowing, protecting, and delineating free speech on American college campuses.

Many of the cases used in this book to illustrate the kinds of struggles speech produces on campuses were resolved, at least initially, in ways that do not reflect the values of inclusive freedom argued for here. Charles Murray was silenced and chased out of Middlebury; Steven Salaita's contract at UIUC was canceled; the

103

Christakis couple left Yale; the University of Chicago sent a letter to freshmen that created a strong backlash; and Missouri failed to recognize the gravity of their students' concerns until drastic steps, including the president's resignation, became necessary.

Some campuses have no clear guidelines to clarify the ways in which various forms of speech may be regulated in their communities, either because they have not faced clashes in this domain or because they mistakenly assume that the general rules and laws apply on campus in ways that make it unnecessary or superfluous to make special campus rules. In fact, campuses house a unique type of community, and their makeup and mission make it necessary to address speech issues up front and to clarify to their members the expectations and rules surrounding speech. This does not mean that campus speech should be more strictly regulated or censored than speech in other public contexts. Rather, it means that with the dual mission of educating and developing new knowledge, speech is even more precious and has an even more significant role to play on campus, which in turn requires that further attention be given to it in handbooks or guidelines and in the practices and expectations of all campus members, beyond what the First Amendment, academic freedom, and other laws and regulations require.

The guidelines and practices that each campus develops can reflect its unique values and its administrative structure and social context. For instance, public and private schools require attention to different legal frameworks; residential and commuter colleges face different needs in the domain of speech; all-girls schools,

schools with specific religious affiliations and missions, research universities, and liberal arts colleges may all have their unique norms, histories, and practices related to speech that can be reflected in their guidelines. But all schools need to think about classrooms and student-sponsored events, about protests and parties, about what is permissible and how they might respond to cases in which community members cross those lines. As I have argued, the values that should inform the guidelines that schools develop in this domain should be informed by inclusive freedom: an unwavering commitment to an inclusive environment that supports speech in all its variety.

Free speech on campus should be viewed neither as a matter of coddling versus intellectual honesty nor as a struggle to protect speech from PC attacks. Rather, current tensions around free speech should be understood as a reflection of the changing mission of colleges, and they should be welcomed and produce an honest reassessment of higher education practices from admissions to pedagogy. Hence considerations beyond constitutional and legal limits should inform the response to tensions around open expression. Protecting intellectual honesty and candor and preserving the substantive opportunity for all campus members to participate in its core mission are the basic currencies of an inclusive campus committed to free expression.

Because the temptation to censor speakers with whom one vehemently disagrees or who are seen as harmful is often strong and because judgment can be clouded by commitment to a cause, it is important for campus rules and expectations to clearly and explicitly protect free speech. While I argued here that even harmful speech should not be censored, outlawed, or strictly regulated on campus, this does not mean that the campus community and its administration have no responsibility to respond or that they have no tools at their disposal. The demands of inclusive freedom on campus are broader than the simple protection of free speech through the institution of rules. The campus is a diverse community of young (and not so young) people, and its missions are to educate them as well as to develop and disseminate knowledge. The acknowledgment of these facts and the recognition that speech can advance these missions by being open and broad or impede them by being exclusive and hurtful should lead to a greater and more detailed focus on the ways the campus community responds to speech. Different stakeholders on campus have different responsibilities and tools to respond to speech. Here are some ways in which the main groups on campus can think about speech and act on a commitment to promote inclusive freedom on campus.

In Class: Instructors and Students

The instructor is primarily responsible for creating an open and inclusive classroom environment where intellectual honesty and accountability is consistently respected and where all can express their perspectives. Planning ahead and considering potential dissent is productive for teaching a good class and for reducing the likelihood of being caught off guard by student responses in ways that can lead to speech suppression or to the class being derailed.

Part of planning can include identifying topics that can hurt or offend some students. Marking those either on the syllabus or in class is a matter of good practice. If students who were personally affected by war as soldiers or civilians get a fair warning about an upcoming discussion about related topics in class or a tough reading on the issue, it expresses respect and compassion on the part of the instructor. It allows these students to participate rather than shut down or avoid class, and it might allow their peers to learn from their experiences and perspectives if they wish to share. If in some cases specific students must be offered alternatives to a particular assignment that they find painful, that too is a prerogative of the instructor and is often simply good pedagogic practice, which allows these students to take the class rather than avoid it altogether.

Instructors would do best to permit and even encourage discussion and debate in class. Engaging with material, including expressions of disagreement, is a more effective way to learn than merely listening. Moreover, expressing one's views can expand the classroom discussion, allowing students and instructors to consider additional experiences, perspectives, or views, and it often enriches the lesson even if it sometimes takes up valuable class time or distracts from the lesson plan.

Inclusive freedom in class does not translate plainly into civility. Both instructors and students who are committed to creating and preserving an atmosphere of inclusive freedom in the classroom have a responsibility to make sure that those in class are not silenced. Assuming that views and ideologies are broadly shared in class can silence those who disagree; disparaging groups can hurt and silence their members—some of whom can be in class, even if unbeknownst to the speaker. The instructor can shape the terms of the discussion, and it is her responsibility to respond to students whose comments risk hurting and silencing others and to do so in a way that preserves the conditions of an open dialogue. Preserving intellectual honesty, accuracy, and commitment to truth will lead the instructor to focus on the lesson and be ready to respond to common inaccuracies or distractions with clarity, both when those oppose the truth (as when challenging scientific fact) and when they are hurtful as well as inaccurate (as with the comment quoted above about affirmative action). Avoiding dignitary harms as a way of preventing the silencing, exclusionary effects of harmful speech requires the instructor to respond not by silencing but by clearly rejecting the view and inviting the speaker to reconsider it when students in class harm each other.

Students in class sometimes encounter instructors who make uncomfortable, insulting, or ideologically charged comments. For example, after the 2016 elections, a few videos circulated in which instructors made disparaging statements about the newly elected president and those who voted for him. However, problematic statements from instructors are not limited to an election season. An instructor in a public health class who notes to his students that they should tell their Mexican friends to stop eating so many burritos because they are exacerbating the obesity epidemic (thus managing to offend people of Mexican descent as well as overweight people) and an instructor in an engineering class who suggests that the women in the room are somehow less capable or were admitted only because of gendered affirmative action or their good looks are everyday examples that regretfully occur on college campuses. While instructors should be advised about the expectations that the college has from them as educators, students too should be empowered to respond when they find their experiences in class to be inappropriate or hurtful. As I have argued, bias reporting systems, which are becoming ubiquitous on college campuses, are not the right way to go. They are unhelpful because they undermine the direct relations between student and instructor, and they are undemocratic because of the chilling effect they have on instructors' speech. What can better be done?

Students have a few avenues for action. The first is to ask themselves if the event requires a response. Was it a slip of tongue? Is the instructor usually respectful or callous? Is there an ongoing feeling of discrimination in this class? Teaching means standing on stage for hours at a time under intense scrutiny. If an instructor makes an unfortunate but uncharacteristic remark, a generous response might be to let it go.

If a student feels offended or uncomfortable regularly in a particular class or if an instructor made a statement that seems deliberate or hurtful to an extent that is hard to ignore, the best course of action would be to address him directly. Confronting hurtful or inappropriate speech is often best done in person and in private after class: "Professor, remember how you said in class that burritos contribute to the obesity epidemic? I felt that it was hurtful to single out one [or, my] ethnic group to talk about a general public health concern that is evident across the population." In most cases, a personal comment along these lines would get the student(s) a heartfelt apology and ideally a retraction of the comment, either right there or in the next class.

If a student feels that she cannot address the instructor in person because she is intimidated or too hurt or because she worries that it will affect the way her performance is assessed in class, she can decide to talk to another member of the academic department or to her advisor. Sharing her concerns is a good way to deliver a message anonymously to the instructor that he is acting in ways that are hurtful to some students.

These responses do just as much (or as little) as bias reporting systems do, but they get there while preserving the educational relations between instructor and student and without chilling speech. Another advantage of these less formal courses of action is that they preserve and enhance the agency of the students. Rather than plugging into a bureaucratic system of forms and anonymous notes, a student can choose a course of action that is more personal and empowering than that offered by a bias reporting system.

Student Groups: Identity and Politics

Student groups, whether organized around a shared identity or a shared political ideology (or a combination of the two), provide the comfort of like-minded peers and friends. Learning to organize, to lead, and to develop and communicate one's views may not be part of the core mission of every college, but at least on residential college campuses, they are central aspects of student life and learning. They also often provide a positive context for befriending new peers, channeling political and civic energies, and creating a vibrant community. Student groups are regularly supported by campus institutions, and campuses should continue that support openly and broadly. Preventing students from organizing around a specific topic, even if it is a contentious one, is almost always not a good decision by a campus administrator because the backlash is regularly worse than the original event and—more significantly—because suppressing speech based on content is undemocratic. Because the campus is not just a part of the public sphere but an educational institution that sometimes has additional missions (for example, religious ones), some campuses can encounter cases in which they could legitimately limit organizing around issues that are in direct contradiction to their expressed mission. In all cases, including the latter ones, expanding the domain of free speech is most often both the democratic and the smart thing to do.

Student groups and their leaders should aim to participate in the educational mission and vision of campus by seeking to engage with each other, with other students, and with the campus overall in democratic, inclusive, and respectful exchanges. When inviting speakers, it is wise to consider the contribution that they can have to campus debate and the extent to which their words and ideas are thoughtful and well-founded, even when they are provocative. Looking to disrupt or enrage can be legitimate goals for an event, but they should be accompanied by content that is worthwhile to think about and consider beyond the spectacle.

Significantly, if any given student group is to have an impact on campus or on policy and society, it should find ways to build coalitions that extend outside their limited identity group or political mission. Collaboration with others who have some overlap with a group's mission or who share an aspect of its goals is a central way to advance a vision. If an identity group is only meant to provide a respite or an outlet to its members, it may find that it does not need to collaborate outside its membership. But if it has any goal to promote, including acceptance of its members on campus, reaching out should be part of its repertoire of actions, even if membership in the group is restricted to students who share a certain identity. Student groups should be open to thinking and acting with others outside the comfort of their own group.

Campus Leaders: Students, Faculty, and Administrators

I began this book by recounting a sit-in by a group of students who decided to stay overnight at an administrative building to demand changes in the university's investment portfolio. As the event was winding down, the faculty and staff members who worked with the student leaders to resolve the matter were back in the office considering the conclusion and any needed next steps (including clean up, though the students diligently cleared the pizza boxes and swept the floor). Our phones buzzed again: a team of outside protesters from a fringe religious group had just marched onto the open walkway at the center of campus, waving signs and chanting antigay slogans. Well-practiced in their particular trade, they were not trespassing or crossing the lines of harassment but stayed just within the boundaries of legality as they advanced their vision of religious and sexual purity and exclusion. This was not their first time on campus, and as per our practice, we dispatched a small team of open expression monitors to observe the situation.

Open Expression Monitors

"Open expression monitors" is a title that frequently provokes shudders and concerned responses from those committed to free speech. But even if the title is less than ideal (and this is the title used at the University of Pennsylvania, changed a few years ago from "open expression observers," which was also unpopular), the role itself is important. Instituting this volunteer opportunity can help administrators distribute knowledge about and responsibility for open expression across campus and thus preserve inclusive freedom. It is practiced in various ways on different campuses, but at its core, this is a volunteer role for faculty, staff, and students who are selected for their conflict-resolution interests and skills and who are trained to ensure the protection of free speech as detailed in the campus guidelines or rules.

Open expression monitors attend events when invited by organizers who are concerned about the possibility of disruption. Their services are advertised on campus and among student groups and other entities that can organize events. When invited, they come to the event wearing large tags identifying their names and their role and generally stand at the back of the event or to the side of a protest. Their role is to diffuse or intervene when anyone's right to express her views freely is limited or blocked by another party. When protesters disrupt a speech or an organized event, the observers approach the protesters and make sure that they are allowed to express their dismay or disagreement as clearly and powerfully as they wish (rather than being shouted down or thrown out). They will also work to ensure that the event can still take place (rather than being shut down by protest). Open expression monitors are community members who wear no uniforms and are only identified by their tags, and they have no authority to provide security services to an event (for example by choosing who gets to come in or who needs to leave). Their role is to support the organizers in making sure that their event proceeds as smoothly as possible while preserving the right to protest by those who object to the event.

Campus leaders should work to incorporate inclusive freedom principles into a variety of issues they confront, from regulations covering events on campus to the way student groups are approved and supported, and from diversity and bias responses to classroom expectations. Free speech monitors are one way for administrators to engage the wider university community in a conversation about inclusion and free speech as it applies to campus.

As we were walking out of the administrative building after the sit-in was resolved, we encountered two open expression monitors standing outside by the antigay protesters. During their previous uninvited visits to campus, the LGBT+ center had set up a table on the other side of the walkway to express their rejection of the message of hate.[1] This time, three young men in feathery scarves were dancing a few feet away, engaged in performance art that included signs, chants, and songs. The monitors mostly stayed to the side, making sure that the walkway remained passable to the throngs of students rushing to class and advising people to avoid direct confrontation with the outsiders. Their mere presence had a calming effect on the potentially explosive scene, and so it remained until the outsiders packed up their signs and megaphones and went on their way.

Toward a Democratic Campus

American campuses are a special part of the democratic public sphere, not mere reflections of it. They are charged with preparing young adults (and older students) for a life of professional opportunities and civic responsibility, leadership, and engagement. Higher education institutions are part of the ladder of mobility even as they screen and exclude many, and they are meant to create a marketplace of ideas, knowledge, and practical skills, all while providing a first (somewhat) independent home to eighteen-year-old high school graduates. Campuses can hardly be expected to reflect democratic practices and ideals without adapting them to their institutional context and goals. Democratic practices should be interpreted in light of the unique and evolving mission that these institutions serve and of the population that uses their services. The democratic accomplishments of college campuses relate directly to their ability to offer true access and opportunity to a diverse group of young adults, and the discussion about free speech protections cannot and should not be disentangled from this broader democratic mission. For campuses to be inclusive and provide all their members with opportunities to develop, express, and communicate their views and perspectives, to expand their knowledge, and to consider the perspectives of others, they need to embrace both inclusion and freedom as guiding principles.

N o t e s

Chapter 1

1. Drabold, Will. 2016. "Read Michelle Obama's Emotional Speech at the Democratic National Convention," *Time*, http://time.com/ 4421538/democratic-convention-michelle-obama-transcript/.

2. Stack, Liam. 2017. "Attack on Alt-Right Leader Has Internet Asking: Is it O.K. to Punch a Nazi?" *New York Times*, https://www.nytimes.com/2017/01/21/us/politics/richard-spencer-punched-attack.html?_r=0.

3. Gallup survey of college students in collaboration with the Knight Foundation and the Newseum Institute, https://www.knightfoundation.org/media/uploads/publication_pdfs/FreeSpeech_campus.pdf.

4. Ibid.

5. *The American Freshman: National Norms Fall 2015*, an annual survey by the Higher Education Research Institute at the University of California, Los Angeles.

6. Mac Donald, Heather. 2017. "Those 'Snowflakes' Have Chilling Effects Even beyond the Campus," *Wall Street Journal*, April 21, https://www.wsj.com/articles/those-snowflakes-have-chilling-effects-even-beyond-the-campus-1492800913.

7. Friedersdorf, Conor. 2016. "The Glaring Evidence That Free Speech Is Threatened on Campus," *The Atlantic*, https://www.theatlantic.com/politics/archive/2016/03/the-glaring-evidence-that-free-speech-is-threatened-on-campus/471825/.

8. "Discord at Middlebury: Students on the Anti-Murray Protests." 2017. *New York Times*, https://www.nytimes.com/2017/03/07/opinion/discord-at-middlebury-students-on-the-anti-murray-protests.html.

9. Adams, Mike. 2015. "Get Out of My Class and Leave America," *Townhall*, https://townhall.com/columnists/mikeadams/2015/08/28/get-out-of-my-class-and-leave-america-n2044785.

10. The protestors at the University of Missouri were embroiled in a free-speech controversy of their own where a college professor aligned with the protestors was caught on video calling for the use of force to remove a student journalist. This professor lost her job.

11. Reilly, Katie. 2016. "University of Chicago Tells Students Not to Expect 'Trigger Warnings' or Safe Spaces," *Fortune*, http://fortune.com/2016/08/25/university-of-chicago-trigger-warnings-safe-spaces/.

12. "Protests Force UC Berkeley to Cancel Milo Yiannopoulos." 2017. *Aljazeera*, http://www.aljazeera.com/news/2017/02/protests-force-uc-berkley-cancel-breitbart-speaker-170202041552305.html.

13. Fuller, Thomas, and Mele, Christopher. 2017. "Berkeley Cancels Milo Yiannopoulos Speech, and Donald Trump Tweets Outrage," *New York Times*, https://www.nytimes.com/2017/02/01/us/uc-berkeley-milo-yiannopoulos-protest.html?_r=0.

14. Svrluga, Susan. 2017. "Trump Threatens UC-Berkeley's Funding after Violent Protests Shut Down a Speaker," *Washington Post*, https://www.washingtonpost.com/local/education/trump-threatens-uc-berkeleys-funding-after-violent-protests-shut-down-a-speaker/2017/02/02/2a13198a-e984-11e6-b82f-687d6e6a3e7c_story.html?utm_term=.281528193ca9.

15. Stein, Perry, and Wan, William. 2017. "How Berkeley Has Become the Far Left and Far Right's Battleground," *Washington Post*, https://www.washingtonpost.com/national/berkeley-at-center-of-political-battleground-reverses-decision-to-cancel-speech-by-conservative-pundit-ann-coulter/2017/04/20/75574a72-25ef-11e7-b503-9d616bd5a305_story.html?utm_term=.8f2498365b96.

16. Jaschik, Scott. 2017. "The Controversial Visit You Didn't Read About," *Inside Higher Ed*, https://www.insidehighered.com/news/2017/03/13/how-controversial-speaker-drew-protests-was-able-give-his-talk-franklin-marshall.

17. U.S. Const. amend. I.

18. Joint Statement on Rights and Freedoms of Students, http://scholarship.law.duke.edu/cgi/viewcontent.cgi?article=4064&context=lcp.

19. The case has further implications beyond this note, see discussion: https://www.britannica.com/topic/Davis-v-Monroe-County -Board-of-Education.

20. For example, the Foundation for Individual Rights in Education (www.thefire.org/).

21. Svrluga, Susan. 2016. "Williams College Cancels a Speaker Who Was Invited to Bring in Provocative Opinions," *Washington Post*, https:// www.washingtonpost.com/news/grade-point/wp/2016/02/20/williams -college-cancels-a-speaker-invited-as-part-of-a-series-designed-to -bring-in-provocative-opinions/?utm_term=.5ab7e69c1253.

22. See discussion in Scott, Joan W. 2015. "The New Thought Police," *The Nation*, April 5, https://www.thenation.com/article/new -thought-police/.

23. Murray, Charles. 2017. "Reflections on the Revolution in Middlebury," *AEIdeas*, http://www.aei.org/publication/reflections-on-the -revolution-in-middlebury/.

24. Weissman, Jordan. 2013. "The Ever-Shrinking Role of Tenured College Professors (in 1 Chart)," *The Atlantic*, https://www.theatlantic .com/business/archive/2013/04/the-ever-shrinking-role-of-tenured -college-professors-in-1-chart/274849/. Note that while tenured professors can rarely be punished for the content of their speech, the share of tenured professors among the faculty is shrinking, while parallel-track instructors, who are not eligible for tenure and whose job security and protections are significantly more limited, are becoming a majority on many campuses. From 1975 to today, the share of tenure and tenure-track professors shrank from around 45 percent of all teaching staff to less than a quarter. As of 2013, part-time faculty accounted for roughly 40 percent of college instructors. Many of these instructors are younger and more of them are women and members of minority groups, so they have a strong incentive to not voice unpopular views.

Chapter 2

1. Friedersdorf, Conor. 2015. "The New Intolerance of Student Activism: A Fight over Halloween Costumes at Yale Has Devolved into an Effort to Censor Dissenting Views," *The Atlantic*, https://www

.theatlantic.com/politics/archive/2015/11/the-new-intolerance-of
-student-activism-at-yale/414810/.

2. Benson, Tessa, and Edwards, Haley Sweetland. 2015. "Exclusive: Yale's Dean Defends 'Safe Spaces' amid Campus Protests," *Time*, http:// time.com/4141125/yale-protests-free-speech/.

3. Foderaro, Lisa W. 2011. "At Yale, Sharper Look at Treatment of Women," *New York Times*, http://www.nytimes.com/2011/04/08/ nyregion/08yale.html.

4. See the report "Guardians of Democracy: The Civic Mission of Schools" at civicmissionofschools.org.

5. Frankenberg, Erica. 2013. "The Role of Residential Segregation in Contemporary School Segregation." *Education and Urban Society* 45: 548–70; Reardon, Sean, and Yun, John. 2002. "Integrating Neighborhoods, Segregating Schools: The Retreat from School Desegregation in the South, 1990–2000." *North Carolina Law Review* 81.

6. The trend of diversity on campus is expected to increase. See Zinshteyn, Mikhail. 2016. "Colleges Face a New Reality as the Number of High School Graduates Will Decline." *Hechinger Report*, December 6, http://hechingerreport.org/colleges-face-new-reality-number-high -schools-graduates-will-decline/.

7. Information from the National Center for Education Statistics: https://nces.ed.gov/fastfacts/display.asp?id=98.

8. A discussion on the growing role of administrators can be found in Zimmerman, Jonathan. 2016. *Campus Politics: What Everyone Needs to Know.* New York: Oxford University Press.

9. Mill, J. S. 1869. *On Liberty*, 4th ed. London: Walter Scott Publishing, 18.

10. Jacobson, D. 2000. "Mill on Liberty, Speech, and the Free Society." *Philosophy and Public Affairs* 29 (3): 276–309.

11. George and West's full statement can be found at: http://jmp .princeton.edu/statement.

12. The "troll problem" cannot readily be resolved by the framework and tools offered here because, for some individuals and groups, the main goal of their speech is to incite hatred, violence, pain, or at the very least a strong angry response. That is the case with the new Open Campus Initiative, a group at Harvard whose stated goal is, "We believe constant action is required to ensure that students never find themselves intimidated by the act of expressing their opinions. Above all, we aim

to ensure that truth will out [*sic*] by actively ensuring this campus is not afraid to hear the views of others." This is also the case with some of the recent violent events at Berkeley. As I argue throughout the book, these difficult cases should not be the main lens to inform the way colleges respond to ongoing issues of speech on their campuses.

13. Muñoz, Vincent Phillip. 2017. "Why I Invited Charles Murray to Speak at Notre Dame," *Real Clear Politics*, http://www.realclearpolitics.com/articles/2017/03/22/why_i_invited_charles_murray_to_speak_at_notre_dame_133401.html.

14. A draft of the bill that was introduced by the Middlebury Student Government Association can be viewed at: https://static1.squarespace.com/static/53a4f9d0e4b0b9f4a3e2b6df/t/58cec4081b10e37dbd6f2ba2/1489945609113/3.12.17+Institutional+Support+in+Public+Events.pdf.

15. The Broken Inquiry blog may be accessed at: https://brokeninquiryblog.wordpress.com/.

16. Ibid.

17. As Justice Brandeis noted in his concurring opinion in *Whitney v. California*, 274 U.S. 357 (1927), "If there be time to expose through discussion the falsehood and fallacies, to avert the evil by the processes of education, the remedy to be applied is more speech, not enforced silence."

18. The Report of the Committee on University Discipline for Disruptive Conduct from the University of Chicago may be viewed in full at: https://provost.uchicago.edu/sites/default/files/documents/reports/ReportCommitteUniversityDisciplineDisruptiveConduct.pdf.

Chapter 3

1. Quoted in Levine, Lawrence W. 1996. *The Opening of the American Mind: Cannons, Culture, and History*. Boston: Beacon Press, 29.

2. See Levy, Jacob T. 2016. "Safe Spaces, Academic Freedom, and the University as a Complex Association," *Bleeding Hearts Libertarians* blog, March 28. http://bleedingheartlibertarians.com/2016/03/safe-spaces-academic-freedom-and-the-university-as-a-complex-association/.

3. Note a concern: College attendance is a predictor of political engagement (see Galston, W. A. 2001. "Political Knowledge, Political

Engagement, and Civic Education." *Annual Review of Political Science* 4 [1]: 217–34), and by providing opportunities for civic development as I recommend here, this inequality would be aggravated. This book focuses on the institutional context of the college and therefore cannot address this significant concern, but I have done that in other work in the K–12 context (for example, Ben-Porath, S. R. 2013. "Deferring Virtue: The New Management of Students and the Civic Role of Schools." *Theory and Research in Education* 11 [2]: 111–28). See also the work from CIRCLE (civicyouth.org) on out-of-college youth.

4. The letter was pulled after the events. It was accessed on March 5, 2017, at https://middleburycampus.com/article/charles -murray-at-middlebury-unacceptable-and-unethical-say-over -450-alumni/.

5. Johnson, Ally. 2016. "Protests Shut Down CIA Director's Talk at Penn," *Daily Pennsylvanian*, http://www.thedp.com/article/2016/04/ protests-shut-down-cia-director-john-brennan-talk.

6. "Discord at Middlebury: Students on the Anti-Murray Protests." 2017. *New York Times*, https://www.nytimes.com/2017/03/07/opinion/ discord-at-middlebury-students-on-the-anti-murray-protests.html.

7. Belkin, Douglas. 2017. "Why the University of Chicago Opposes 'Trigger Warnings': President Robert Zimmer on the Role of Universities and Why They Need to Be Open to Controversial Ideas," *Wall Street Journal*, February 20, 2017, https://www.wsj.com/articles/ why-the-university-of-chicago-opposes-trigger-warnings-1487646602.

8. Quotes from both students are from Jaschik, Scott. 2016. "The Chicago Letter and Its Aftermath," *Inside Higher Ed*, https://www .insidehighered.com/news/2016/08/29/u-chicago-letter-new-students -safe-spaces-sets-intense-debate.

9. Waldron, Jeremy. 2014. *The Harm in Hate Speech*. Cambridge: Harvard University Press.

10. Ibid., 166.

11. See Steele, C. M., and Aronson, J. 1995. "Stereotype Threat and the Intellectual Test Performance of African Americans." *Journal of Personality and Social Psychology* 69 (5) and a summary of research: http:// www.apa.org/research/action/stereotype.aspx.

12. Fricker, Miranda. 2007. *Epistemic Injustice: Power and the Ethics of Knowing*. Oxford: Oxford University Press.

13. For discussion on teaching LGBTQ students and instructive tools for inclusive education more broadly, see Mayo, Cris. 2013. *LGBTQ Youth and Education: Politics and Practices.* New York: Teachers College Press.

14. Izadi, Elahe. 2015. "The Incidents That Led to the University of Missouri President's Resignation," *Washington Post*, https://www.washingtonpost.com/news/grade-point/wp/2015/11/09/the-incidents-that-led-to-the-university-of-missouri-presidents-resignation/?utm_term=.6965bb82f04d.

15. Ibid.

16. Ibid.

17. Ibid.

18. Both quotes are from Joan W. Scott's "The New Thought Police" (see note 22 to chapter 1, above), in which she raises an important set of concerns about civility as an impediment to free speech.

19. Redden, Elizabeth. 2017. "Pro-Palestinian Group Banned on Political Grounds," *Inside Higher Ed*, https://www.insidehighered.com/news/2017/01/18/fordham-denies-student-palestinian-rights-group-approval-being-too-polarizing; https://www.insidehighered.com/sites/default/server_files/files/EldredgetoSJP_12-22-16_Decision_Redacted.pdf.

20. "Freedom of Speech for Fordham Students?" 2017. *The Faculty Lounge*, http://www.thefacultylounge.org/2017/01/freedom-of-speech-for-fordham-students.html. The opposition to SJP claimed that the petitioning students acted with aggression. I do not discuss the full case here but rather refer to the two positions as quoted to illustrate the argument about civility.

21. Harris, F. C. 2014. "The Rise of Respectability Politics." *Dissent* 61 (1): 33–37.

22. "Yale to Change Calhoun College's Name to Honor Grace Murray Hopper." 2017. *Yale News*, http://news.yale.edu/2017/02/11/yale-change-calhoun-college-s-name-honor-grace-murray-hopper-0.

23. Stack, Liam, and Fisher, Gabriel. 2015. "Princeton Agrees to Consider Removing a President's Name," *New York Times*, https://www.nytimes.com/2015/11/20/nyregion/princeton-agrees-to-consider-removing-a-presidents-name.html. The name was not changed in this instance.

24. Bejan, Teresa. 2017. *Mere Civility: Disagreement and the Limits of Toleration*. Cambridge: Harvard University Press.

25. Other democratic practices and structures beyond free speech similarly require rethinking in light of digital advancement. See Reidenberg, Joel. Forthcoming. *Digitocracy*. New Haven: Yale University Press.

26. Cohen, Jodi S. 2015. "University of Illinois OKs $875,000 Settlement to End Steven Salaita Dispute," *Chicago Tribune*, http://www.chicagotribune.com/news/local/breaking/ct-steven-salaita-settlement-met-20151112-story.html.

27. Flaherty, Coleen. 2016. "Suspended for Anti-Semitism," *Inside Higher Ed*, https://www.insidehighered.com/news/2016/08/04/months-later-oberlin-suspends-professor-who-made-anti-semitic-remarks-facebook.

28. Lazar, Kay, and Rosen, Andy. 2016. "Amherst College Suspends Men's Cross Country over Offensive Posts," *Boston Globe*, https://www.bostonglobe.com/metro/2016/12/12/amherst-college-suspends-men-cross-country-due-racist-misogynist-and-homophobic-messages/xOhcJ4K0AJ1013UCaTapaM/story.html; Whelan, Tim, Jr. 2017. "Hockey Captain in Alaska Suspended for Racist, Homophobic Tweets," *USA Today*, http://usatodayhss.com/2017/hockey-captain-in-alaska-suspended-for-racist-homophobic-tweets; "University of Kansas Cheerleaders Suspended over KKK Snapchat Pic." 2016. *CBS News*, http://www.cbsnews.com/news/university-of-kansas-cheer-squad-members-suspended-for-kkk-snapchat-pic/.

29. See Dishon, Gideon, and Ben-Porath, Sigal. "Beyond Trolling: Educating for Digital Civility" (unpublished manuscript).

Chapter 4

1. Eagan, Kevin, Ellen Bara Stolzenberg, Jennifer Berdan Lozano, Melissa C. Aragon, Maria Ramirez Zuchard, and Sylvia Hurtado. 2014. "Undergraduate Teaching Faculty: The 2013–2014 HERI Faculty Survey," *Higher Education Research Institute at UCLA*, https://heri.ucla.edu/monographs/HERI-FAC2014-monograph.pdf.

2. Pierson, James, and Schaffer Riley, Naomi. 2017. "The Liberal Arts Bubble Didn't Always Cause Such Trouble." *Wall Street Journal*, March 10, https://www.wsj.com/articles/the-liberal-arts-bubble-didnt-always-cause-such-trouble-1489187214.

3. Suk, J. 2014. "The Trouble with Teaching Rape Law." *The New Yorker* 15: 12–14. The article relies on a few anecdotes but suggests that they relate to a broader phenomenon.

4. Reilly, Katie. 2016. "University of Chicago Tells Students Not to Expect 'Trigger Warnings' or Safe Spaces," *Fortune*, http://fortune.com/2016/08/25/university-of-chicago-trigger-warnings-safe-spaces/. The letter continued, "We do not cancel invited speakers because their topics might prove controversial and we do not condone the creation of intellectual 'safe spaces' where individuals can retreat from ideas and perspectives at odds with their own." These additional issues were discussed in the previous chapter.

5. "Letter: Faculty Respond to Ellison with a Letter of Their Own." 2016. *Chicago Maroon*, https://www.chicagomaroon.com/article/2016/9/13/letter-faculty-respond-ellison-letter/.

6. For a discussion of the role of teaching controversial issues to enhance civic skills, see Hess, Diana, and MacAvoy, Paula. 2014. *The Political Classroom: Evidence and Ethics in Democratic Education.* Abingdon: Routledge.

7. See Kelly, Erin I. 2015. "Modeling Justice in Higher Education." *The Aims of Higher Education.* Edited by Harry Brighouse and Michael McPherson. Chicago: University of Chicago Press, 135–55.

8. France, D. 2016. *How to Survive a Plague: The Inside Story of How Citizens and Science Tamed AIDS.* New York: Knopf.

9. Callan, E. 2016. "Education in Safe and Unsafe Spaces." *Philosophical Inquiry in Education* 24 (1): 64–78.

10. Anderson, E. S. 1995. "The Democratic University: The Role of Justice in the Production of Knowledge." *Social Philosophy and Policy* 12 (2): 186–219.

11. Callan, E. 2011. "When to Shut Students Up: Civility, Silencing, and Free Speech." *Theory and Research in Education* 9 (1): 3–22. Callan prefers to err on the side of intellectual candor rather than to risk uncharitable interpretation of a student's comment.

Conclusion

1. Fulghieri, Carl-Emmanuel, and Sorantino, Lauren. 2016. "Preachers on College Green Rail against 'Homo Sex,' Students Respond," *Daily Pennsylvanian*, http://www.thedp.com/article/2016/09/preachers-college -green-homosexuality-protest.

Acknowledgments

In some ways, this book was a family project. My family has heard me speak endlessly about free speech on campus since I began chairing Penn's Committee on Open Expression. The idea for writing this book came from Noah, who also helped in myriad other ways from testing out ideas to copyediting. My love and gratitude cannot be expressed on paper. My parents Shlomit and Peleg's loving support, as always, was vital. My children, Itamar and Amalia, read this work and engaged with me in insightful exchanges about resistance and free thought. I hope you both continue to speak your minds on and off campus.

I am grateful to Anne Barnhill and our colleagues at Penn's Ethics Breakfast for thinking with me early on and to the *Journal of Constitutional Law*'s annual meeting for inviting me to participate in a lively panel on this topic. Kevin McDonough invited me to write a comment on Eamonn Callan's important article on this topic in *Philosophical Inquiries in Education*, which got me started on writing about free speech when up until then I had mostly been worrying about it.

A number of friends and colleagues helped me think about these matters. Joan Goodman always challenges me to think and rethink and also read the full manuscript generously and critically. I benefitted immensely from conversations with and advice from Anita Allen, Suzi Dovi, Ellen Goodman, Hikaru Kozuma, Jacob T. Levy, Lisa Liebman, Rogers Smith, and Mary Summers. Damon Linker provided great editorial help.

I am grateful to my excellent research assistants, Jasmine Blanks Jones and Jacquelyn Greiff (and Charlotte!).

Finally, while chairing Penn's Committee on Open Expression was not without its challenges, it provided me with ample opportunities to think and rethink my views on the many issues surrounding free speech on campus. I'm grateful to the students, colleagues, and administrators who took part in this process by engaging in the lively exchange of ideas at Penn and who will surely continue to challenge me in the future.